CHELTENHAM'S
RACING HEROES

P E T E R   G I L L

SUTTON PUBLISHING

First published in the United Kingdom in 1998 by
Sutton Publishing Limited · Phoenix Mill
Thrupp · Stroud · Gloucestershire · GL5 2BU

British Library Cataloguing in Publication Data

A catalogue record for this book is available from the British Library

ISBN 0-7509-2044-0

 TM ALAN SUTTON™ and SUTTON™ are the
trade marks of Sutton Publishing Limited

Typeset in 11/12 pt Ehrhardt.
Typesetting and origination by
Sutton Publishing Limited.
Printed in Great Britain by
Ebenezer Baylis, Worcester.

Contents

*To my father who has those most notable of heroic qualities,
determination and strength, which have enabled him to attain
beyond what his natural talents and opportunities would have
predicted. It is the privilege and responsibility of all fathers that if
to no-one else they are a hero to their children.*

Introduction

All this life is one great gamble - when you are in the limelight everyone wants you - but when disaster or bad luck comes your way - they 'blank out'.

Campbell Russell

As we move into the twenty-first century it seems likely that Cheltenham will remain the 'Home of National Hunt Racing' for the foreseeable future. It richly deserves this title for the rich spectacle of racing it puts on at Prestbury Park each March in its festival. Nowhere in the world is there such high-class racing over three full days in such an auditorium as there is at Cheltenham in the spring. The Grand National at Aintree will always be a race out on its own for without doubt the winners, both human and equine, do need strength and stamina to gain victory, but the race has always been and remains something of a lottery. The field is so big, the course so long and the jumps so testing that all the horses can be impeded by a dozen imponderables. At Cheltenham the winners of the races are much more consistently those horses and jockeys with the most class and ability. The races are far more often (though not always) won on merit, and thus Cheltenham winners read like a galaxy of racing stars.

However, as we can marvel at Cheltenham's status today as National Hunt's home we do so purely on the basis of a few days of excellent racing each year at the racecourse. It is easily forgotten that in the not so distant past Cheltenham was truly the home of racing with trainers, jockeys and owners proliferating all around. It could easily be argued that had racing not adopted Cheltenham with such energy and enthusiasm then the town would never have overcome the severe slump it suffered after the interest in its spa waters had waned.

From the beginning of the nineteenth century there were the jockeys and trainers of Grand National and Grand Annual Steeplechase winners present and forging the embryonic development of racing at Cheltenham. During a halcyon period from the early 1920s to the 1960s there were top jockeys living all around the town, along with top trainers and dozens of less accomplished jockeys, trainers and apprentices.

This book is about just a handful of these racing greats. There are many more – equally heroic, equally accomplished – that I would have loved to include; possibly they will feature in a sister publication. People such as George Stevens, the record five-time winner of the Grand National who lived on Cleeve Hill and died in a racing accident in Southam at the age of thirty-eight; Thomas

Pickernell, the ex-Cheltenham College boy who rode in a staggering seventeen Grand Nationals, winning on three occasions; William Holman, the winning jockey of the Grand Annual Steeplechase on three occasions and the winning trainer of three Grand Nationals; Charlie Piggott, the trainer of African Sister, the Champion Hurdle winner of 1939; John Roberts, who trained Four Ten to win the Cheltenham Gold Cup from his stables in Prestbury; Alf Newey, who trained at Woodmancote, having ridden to success in the 1907 Grand National; Arthur Saxby, who rode successfully over jumps before turning to training in Bishops Cleeve – and of course The Duke, David Nicholson, successful jockey and twice Champion Trainer and winning trainer of the 1988 Gold Cup with Charter Party.

The subjects I have chosen for this book all reached the pinnacle of their sport. Some had natural talent to aid them to the top, others had grit and determination. They came from varied backgrounds and, apart from the lives of Billy Speck and Billy Stott which mirrored each other tragically closely, are all very different. There are both National Hunt and flat race men here, and successful jockeys as well as successful trainers. Together they give a small hint of the importance Cheltenham has had on the development and history of racing in general.

Everyone needs heroes, people to look up to and admire – if not to admire all aspects of their life or accomplishments, certainly to have some element to respect. In today's world there are far too few heroes. In a time when increasingly money is a god, Campbell Russell's inscription which was written over sixty years ago is sadly more true today than it was then: 'when you are in the limelight everyone wants you – but when disaster or bad luck comes your way they "blank out"'. Therefore I put forward these men as some of my racing heroes. I respect them all and admire what they achieved in their lives. Some I admire more than others, but each has attained something to be proud of and that we can respect.

From the Victorian age, Fred Archer, the most successful jockey of his period and, had death not come so soon, he would surely have put down racing records that wouldn't have been broken by either Gordon Richards or Lester Piggott.

Then there is a collection of jockeys who made Cheltenham their home between the wars, mainly because there were many trainers such as Saxby, Newey and Ben Roberts in this area who were offering and booking rides. It is these characters who really turned the Cheltenham area into a racing community similar to that of Lambourn and Newmarket. These are the two Billys – Speck and Stott, Tim Hamey, Frenchie Nicholson, Gerry Wilson and Davy Jones. They all lived in the region during this period and between them they amassed thirteen jockey championships, six Gold Cups, four Champion Hurdles and two Grand Nationals. These men were friends and contemporaries, and it was their success that did so much for the racing community as a whole around Cheltenham's villages. Four of them had success both on the flat and over the jumps and one of them, Davy Jones, had the audacity to ride under both codes of racing, year in, year out.

It is no coincidence that the success of some of these jockeys, Stott, Wilson and Nicholson in particular, is inextricably linked to one of racing's most memorable characters – Dorothy Paget and her great stable stars, in particular Golden Miller and Insurance. These three men shared many of their successes and failures with the Hon. Miss Paget, and their stories combined give the story of Golden Miller and Dorothy Paget. Many of the highlights of Billy Speck's story are in running second best to the Miller. Stott and Wilson were acclaimed and respected champions of their profession. They brought Paget great success with Golden Miller and Insurance but both ended their association with her under clouds of bitterness and discontent. Nicholson rode for her and even went on to train for her, and probably shared with her the best relationship she ever had with a jockey and trainer. Billy Speck inevitably rode against her horses and although partnered with some of the best and himself undoubtedly one of the best, it was his misfortune that he was racing in the same age as such wonderful horses.

The remaining three personalities enjoyed their success in the latter half of the century. Paul Cook set the world alight as an apprentice flat race jockey; turning professional his career suffered until he pushed himself back to the top by sheer determination and belief. Jim Wilson rode as an amateur during his whole racing career, and was regarded as one of the best amateurs of his day. When he won the 1981 Gold Cup on Little Owl he became the first amateur to do it for over thirty years and to date is the last amateur to have achieved it.

Richard Pitman, who was born in Cheltenham during the Second World War, was perhaps the least naturally gifted of the jockeys here. Some would say – himself probably among them – that his success was born from luck and by having ridden some of the best horses ever to have raced in England. Without a doubt he got to ride the best of a generation. However, what Richard Pitman did was scale the ladder of success through some talent, some luck and a great deal of determination and hard work. There are plenty of talented people around in all aspects of life who achieve nothing with their talent, or fail to achieve as much as they could because they haven't the dedication, work ethic or commitment. Often these are the harshest critics of those less gifted individuals who have worked harder than them and surpassed them. Yet to achieve heights above natural capability is surely something to be truly admired, regardless of the field, and it is perhaps these qualities shown by Richard Pitman that are most to be admired.

Heroes are normal men who give us something to look up to; they are the ones who fuel our ambitions. All of these men had qualities that we can admire and possibly gain from; in their own right they are all heroes. Perhaps where normality is most in evidence we can get the greatest sense of inspiration – if heroes are indeed unexceptional people who became exceptional then there is hope for all of us.

Acknowledgements

I would like to give the most sincere thanks to the following people, without whom this book would not have been possible. The generosity of those who gave their time so willingly to help me, permitted me into their homes and allowed me the perusal and use of their cherished scrapbooks and photographs never ceases to amaze me. I am deeply indebted to them and hope above all that this book meets with their approval.

Dr S. Blake and the Cheltenham Art Gallery and Museum; all at the Cheltenham Reference Library; Mr P. Cook; Mr and Mrs J. Hamey; Mr R. Harrison; Mrs J. Holmes; Mr P. Jones; Peter McNeile and Judy McGill of the Cheltenham Racecourse; Mr and Mrs D. Nicholson; Mr B. Parkin; Mr R. Pitman; Miss M. Pitman; Mr and Mrs Malcolm Smith; Mr G. Snelling and the National Horseracing Museum; Mr W. Stott; Mrs M. Rimell; Mr A.J. Wilson.

Every effort has been made to confirm the identity of the copyright holders of all the photographs. It is hoped that any omissions will be excused.

1

Fred Archer

The most successful jockey in the history of British flat racing is Sir Gordon Richards, who between 1920 and 1954 rode a staggering 4,870 winners from 21,843 mounts; he was champion jockey twenty-six times and won fourteen Classics. His tally of 269 winners in 1947 remains a record.

The jockey with most Classic wins is Lester Piggott with thirty, the first being when at the age of eighteen he took the 1954 Derby on Never Say Die and the last almost forty years later when in 1992 he won the 2000 Guineas on Rodrigo de Triano. He won his first race on a horse called The Chase in the Wigan Lane Selling Handicap at the age of twelve in 1948, and in a racing career that spanned five decades was champion jockey eleven times. He ranks as the second most successful British jockey ever.

His life tragically cut short when just twenty-nine years of age, Frederick James Archer had been champion jockey for thirteen successive years – a record that has never been equalled. Of his 8,004 mounts he rode an incredible 2,748 winners, a statistic better than 1 in 3, of which twenty-one were Classic wins. When Sir Gordon Richards was twenty-nine he had been champion just seven times and Lester Piggott had at that age just gained three titles. Had he lived, it is hard to believe that Fred Archer would not have set down a record superior to Sir Gordon Richards', especially when you consider that Archer's career was in fact just half as long as that of Britain's premier jockey.

Fred Archer was born into the racing world on 11 January 1857 at St George's Cottages, St George's Place, Cheltenham. This piece of land had originally been acquired in 1815 by his paternal grandfather, William, who was a carpenter by trade but was listed as a milk-seller in the census of 1841, and had turned part of his land to use as livery stables. Fred Archer's father, also named William, was born in 1826 and soon developed a love of horse-riding, so much so that at the age of eleven he ran away from home to join a trainer named Eccles, based in Birmingham. Initially his flat-racing career was a promising one with enough winners to sustain him. After a while however the effort of keeping his weight down became too much and he turned his attention to the developing sport of steeplechasing, at which he showed sufficient skill to come to the attention of Tsar Nicholas I of Russia. At the age of seventeen William Archer was offered by the tsar and duly accepted the position of looking after his stud and riding his horses. For two years he maintained this employment and then, perhaps due to home-sickness or the adverse climate, William returned to Cheltenham where he

41 St George's Place, Cheltenham, the birthplace of Frederick James Archer.

met Emma Hayward, the daughter of the landlord of The Kings Arms in Prestbury. On 12 February 1850 they were married and moved to St George's Cottages. Here all but one of their five children were born. Their last, Charles Edward, was born on 22 December 1858, by which time they had moved to Prestbury. Earlier that year William Archer had won the Grand National on the William Holman-trained Little Charley – Holman was a Prestbury-based trainer at this time and is the great-great-grandfather of twice-champion trainer David Nicholson.

Initially the family lived at Cintra House (now Vine Tree Cottage) on the corner of Mill Street and The Burgage in Prestbury, then in 1861 William Archer succeeded his father-in-law as landlord of The Kings Arms and the following year he rode his last race on a horse called Little Dwarf at a race meeting in Beckford.

All three Archer sons were taught by their father to ride, but it was the middle one, Fred, who showed the greatest aptitude. Fred's first recorded race came in 1865 when at the age of eight he rode his pony named Chard against a youth on a donkey around a course marked out behind The Plough Inn in Prestbury. Fred was beaten by a head and was inconsolable. Nevertheless his determination to win brought him to race in a donkey race also at The Plough and this became his first recorded triumph. During the next three years Fred often rode out hunting with his father and clearly began to show great promise. On the recommendation of a friend, William Archer wrote to the Newmarket trainer Mathew Dawson to ask whether he would take Fred on as an apprentice. In February 1868 when he was just eleven years old, Fred, accompanied by his father, went to Mat Dawson's racing stables at Heath House in Newmarket. His father stayed with him for a week while the trainer assessed the boy's merits, and then on the 10th of the month apprenticeship papers were drawn up and signed that would effectively make Archer junior the responsibility of Dawson for the next five years. According to this document the lad had to be prepared to serve his master at any time, day or night, not gamble, go to taverns or get married – among other stipulations. Apart

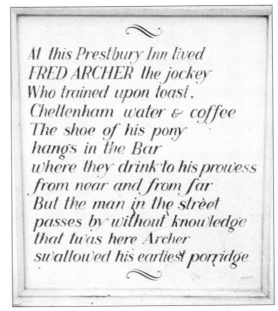

The plaque on the wall outside The Kings Arms in Prestbury, home of Fred Archer during his earliest years.

from the valuable apprenticeship that the aspiring jockey would serve he would earn wages of seven guineas for his first year, nine for his second, eleven for his third and thirteen for his fourth and fifth years.

By all accounts Fred Archer was fortunate to be given such a position. Mathew Dawson was a greatly respected trainer and had many written requests from young jockey hopefuls. He had already trained Sunbeam to win the 1858 St Leger and Thormanby the 1860 Derby. His patrons included the Duke of Hamilton, the Duke of Newcastle, the Duke of Portland and later, most famously, Lord Falmouth.

Dawson could be described as a hard man who drove his apprentices as hard as he drove himself. His love was not for money but for winning races, and to this end he was devoted and determined. However, in time Archer would hold a place in Dawson's heart akin to that of a son – Dawson would never have a son of his own, and in many ways as their futures developed together there was a bond that was very much that of father and son.

On 14 October 1869 Fred rode in his first public race on a horse named Honoria in the Newmarket Town Plate. The horse had been put into the race by Dawson to make the running for another of his horses, Stromboli, owned by Lord Falmouth. Fred rode to his orders and consequently finished last; Stromboli, ridden by Fred Webb, won the race and both trainer and owner were pleased with the day's result. Lord Falmouth had moved his horses to Mathew Dawson earlier that year and in the years to come the triumvirate of Archer, Falmouth and

Dawson would become synonymous with success in the racing field – each being critical to the others' success.

A month after his first public ride, Fred Archer rode his first winner. Aged twelve and weighing just 4 stone 11 lb, he took Maid of Trent to victory in a steeplechase at Bangor for a Mrs Willan. Curiously, the jockey that would have such flat-racing success notched up his first winner under any kind of rules in a steeplechase – it would be ten months later on 28 September 1870 at Chesterfield that the young Archer would ride his first winner on the flat. The horse was named Athol Daisy and belonged to a Mr Bradley, and was trained at Malton by John Peart. Just over two weeks later Archer would notch up his second victory on the flat by taking the Tay Handicap on Lincoln Lass in the Caledonian Hunt Meeting.

At the end of his second year of apprenticeship he had succeeded in riding in public for the first time and then ridden another fourteen mounts, securing two wins on the flat and one over jumps. The following year, 1871, he had forty rides but could only convert three of them into wins, and suffered for the first and only time in his career the ignominy of being punished by the racing stewards and being suspended from racing for two weeks for misconduct at the post.

Then in 1872 he began to get a greater volume of rides, one hundred and eighty in total, of which he took a respectable twenty-seven first past the post, including on 8 October Salvanos to win the Cesarewitch. It is impressive that Archer, still only fifteen and an apprentice, was respected enough by Mat Dawson to be given the ride in such an important race, especially as the horse was known to need strong handling.

In the February of the following year he completed his apprenticeship and was appointed by Dawson as lightweight jockey at the Heath House Stables, and soon began to command the respect of his peers and the interest of all racing fans.

In time his intelligence and determination to win were recognised. He was unusually tall for a flat race jockey and not regarded as the most accomplished or stylish rider of his day – both George Fordham and Tom Cannon were regarded as his superiors in that field – but he would pay very great attention to form and always left a race knowing how well the other runners had raced. Frequently if he liked a horse that he had just beaten he would track down its owner and ask to be given the ride next time, believing that he could make the difference between an also-ran and a winner. Flattered that anyone should have faith in their horse, owners would often be quite willing to give the ride to him, and as his fame grew and the tally of his winners increased his requests were met with increasing appreciation and a great deal of respect.

From his earliest races, Archer's determination to win was often at the expense of his poor mount and in a style that would not be accepted today. His horses would frequently come home bleeding from spur and whip wounds as he would aim to get every last bit of effort from them. But he got results and the unmerciful manner in which he often obtained those results was ignored or accepted as necessary. It is most unlikely that he had affection for the poor animals that he rode, otherwise he couldn't have been as brutal as he clearly was, but he had a natural talent for horsemanship and for mastering his mounts; furthermore he would often verbally bully other riders during a race to force his way through. Yet away from the track he was renowned as a quiet, impeccably dressed, sensitive man who never allowed the fame and fortune that became his to affect his manner.

The year 1874 saw the emergence of Archer as the great jockey that he surely was. On 6 May he won his first of twenty-one Classics, the 2000 Guineas on Lord Falmouth's Atlantic. By all accounts the colt was not expected to win and started the race at odds of 10–1. Archer timed the race perfectly and pushed him home to win by a neck. By the end of the year Archer was crowned champion jockey with 147 wins from 530 mounts, a title that he would not relinquish during his lifetime and a tally of winners that he would never fall below. As well as that first Classic, included among the winners in his first championship year were F. Swindell's Tomahawk in the Lincoln Handicap, Lord Wilton's Modwena in the Stewards' Cup at Goodwood, Lord Falmouth's Repentance in the Clearwell Stakes – a race that he would go on to win for the following three seasons and eight times in total – and another of Lord Falmouth's mounts, Lady Love in the Woodcote Stakes.

With success came inevitably demands both on his finances and, as he attempted to consolidate his success and improve on it, his health. As he became more and more successful his parents began to lean on him more and more to subsidise their cost of living. Never very careful with money, William Archer used his son's increasingly famous name to get credit and Fred dutifully and generously saw that his parents didn't go short. William and Emma Archer had left The Kings Arms in Prestbury in or around 1873 and moved to The Rose and Crown in Cheltenham's High Street; shortly afterwards Fred set up his father as the landlord of The Andoversford Hotel in Andoversford. Another burden on his finances was the fact that Fred was a heavy and largely unsuccessful gambler, even occasionally betting against his own mounts in races – a practice that was allowed at that time – but although he was later accused of stopping horses and race fixing, he rarely raced without the intention of winning and often won a race at the cost of his own wager.

In 1874 Fred Archer was still doing weights of 6 stone or less, but as the year progressed and he began to reach his true and eventual height of 5 feet 8½ inches, he began to find it more and more difficult and eventually impossible to sustain his weight at such a minimum. As a consequence he began a regime of Turkish baths, a starvation diet and a purgative concoction developed by his Newmarket doctor dubbed 'Archer's mixture' that clearly was somewhat to blame for his premature death. Even when he became first jockey at Heath House Stables in 1875 and was thus able to take rides that were not at the lower end of the handicap he purged himself to extreme. Nevertheless, after 1878 he was unable to manage a weight under 8 stone 7 lb with any consistency. In fact when not racing in the winter months his weight would increase to what must be assumed as its natural level of around 11 stone. Thus he was always forcing his body to accept a weight perhaps 2½ stone below what it should have been. His racing diet consisted of a tablespoonful of castor oil and half an orange for breakfast, and a glass of champagne and a sardine for dinner.

In 1874 this punishing regime on his physique was in its infancy, but as the years went by and he found it more and more difficult to drop his weight, so he worked harder and harder to do so. Perhaps it is surprising that he lived as long as he did.

The following year saw Archer claim his second Classic winner on the Lord Falmouth-owned mare Spinaway in the 1000 Guineas, and then on the same horse his third Classic in The Oaks and also the Yorkshire Oaks. It was the year that Lord Falmouth took out a retainer on his services and the triumvirate of Falmouth, Archer and Dawson was cemented. In that same year he won for Lord Falmouth the Champagne Stakes and the Clearwell Stakes on Farnese, and the Chesterfield Stakes on Skylark. For Captain Prime he won the Stewards' Cup on Trappist and for R. Howett the Liverpool Autumn Cup on Activity.

There were no Classics coming Archer's way in 1876, but he won his second Cesarewitch, this time on J. Smith's Rosebery, his first of four Queen's Vases with Thunder, owned by H.F.C. Vyner, and on the same horse the City and Suburban Handicap; for Lord Falmouth the Champagne Stakes on Lady Golightly and the Clearwell Stakes on Silvio. He also broke the two hundred barrier of winners for the first time in notching up a tally of 207 wins from 662 mounts; he would repeat this feat another seven times in his short career, the best tally coming in 1885 when he notched up 246 wins – a record that lasted until 1933 when Gordon Richards broke it on his way to 259 wins. In 1947 Gordon Richards set the record of wins in a season to 269; this still stands today.

The next season he really began to reel in the big races: the Queen's Vase, York Cup, Yorkshire Oaks, Great Eastern Handicap, City and Suburban Handicap, Criterion Stakes, Gimcrack Stakes, Clearwell Stakes, Richmond Stakes, Chesterfield Stakes and Prendergast Stakes were all his, and to cap it all he won his first of an eventual five Derbys when he brought Lord Falmouth's Silvio home by half a length from Glen Arthur. On the same horse he took the St Leger – a race he would go on to win six times.

At just twenty years of age Fred Archer had won all the English Classics and been crowned champion jockey for four successive years. Furthermore on 19 April 1877 he had won all six races in which he had mounts on a seven racecard at Newmarket, a feat that he would later duplicate at Lewes on 5 August 1882. He was at the pinnacle of his sport, famous beyond racing and wealthy beyond his wildest dreams. He was surely the golden boy of his time and it seemed as though it would just get better.

Unfortunately, fate often deals a savage blow and Fred Archer was destined to suffer his fair share of tragedy. On Saturday 23 March 1878 William Archer junior, Fred's older brother, died from injuries sustained when he fell from his mount Salvanic in a hurdle race held at Prestbury the previous day. Ironically Fred's other brother Charles had ridden the same horse on the Thursday to finish third in a selling hurdle race and then went on to win the Cheltenham Grand Annual Steeplechase on Duellist the same day. Fred had always remained close to his family and grieved terribly the loss of his brother.

In the saddle for the 1878 season he won The Oaks, St Leger and the Yorkshire Oaks on Jannette for Lord Falmouth, but his weight was becoming an increasing problem and it was at this time that he began to take his 'mixture'.

Archer's success in the saddle was heralded throughout the country and along with Gloucestershire's other great sporting son of the period, W.G. Grace, was surely one of the first of sport's icons. The inevitability of him winning was such that a catchphrase adopted at the time was 'Archer's Up!' – if Archer was in the saddle then the winner was a foregone conclusion, and statistically this comes very near to being correct. He was regularly averaging better than one win from every three mounts and in 1884 he achieved the remarkable average of one win to every 2.39 rides. His success didn't diminish his appetite for winners though; he would travel the length and breadth of the country in his pursuit of victories and even crossed the Channel to France, where he won the Grand Prix de Paris on three occasions (1882 on Bruce, 1885 on Paradox and 1886 on Minting) and the Prix du Jockey Club (French Derby) twice (1880 on Beauminet and 1883 on Frontin). On the whole, though, he didn't enjoy racing in France as he believed, probably rightly, that the jockeys conspired to run a hard race against him and that the crowds were always against him. On one occasion he rode at The Curragh in Ireland.

The seeds of tragedy were slowly germinating as the new decade approached, but to all spectators it still seemed that Fred Archer could do no wrong. In 1880 he won his second Derby, this time on Bend Or owned by the Duke of Westminster. This was an extraordinary race, not just in the close finish that prevailed between Archer and Tom Cannon on Robert the Devil, but in the fact that four weeks before the race Archer had been severely savaged by a colt named Muley Edris while working him at Heath House. The colt grabbed Archer by the arm after he had dismounted to move some obstacles and set about destroying the limb. The mutilation that resulted made the arm next to useless, the muscles were intensely damaged and for a while it seemed that no matter what dressings the doctor put on nothing would help it. Archer was unable to ride and the arm seemed unable to heal quickly enough. Nevertheless when Derby Day approached he insisted that he was fit enough and able enough to take the ride on Bend Or. The Duke with much consternation agreed to let him ride and with a pad in his palm and a piece of iron wrapped on to the arm within his jacket, Archer rode the race of his life. Bend Or was not expected to beat Robert the Devil and the fact that he did by just a nose and with Archer in obvious pain is testament to his skills of horsemanship, bravery and commitment to win.

In 1881 Mathew Dawson made Archer a partner in Heath House Stables and with retainers for his services from Lord Falmouth, Lord Hastings, the Duke of Portland, the Duke of Westminster and Lord Alington he was at the top of his tree. He had his own string of horses and was the owner of land. On 1 June of that year he won the Derby for the third time, this time on Iroquois, the first American horse to win the race, owned by Mr Lorillard (who didn't manage to cross the Atlantic to see the race) and trained in England by an American named Jacob Pincus. He then found himself falling in love with Mat Dawson's niece, Helen Rose Dawson, and once their engagement was confirmed he set about building a home of impressive proportions for his bride-to-be. Falmouth House in Newmarket, named after his great patron, was begun in 1882 and it soon weighed heavily on the jockey's purse. Even though his earnings were now very considerable, the ever-increasing cost of this building venture became a concern to

Fred Archer in the colours of Lord Hastings.

him, his gambling was still heavy and the demands of his parents for funds were unceasing. He was under the constant pressure of keeping his weight down, and Mathew Dawson insisted that he took an active role in the stables where Fred was a partner, added to which there were the first whispers of race-fixing allegations being heard against him.

It is a British affliction that an individual's success is often met with contempt, winners are ultimately reviled and smears against those that have made good are met with open arms. Such was the case with Fred Archer when suggestions that he threw races began to surface. It will never be known whether Archer transgressed or not, but the fact that he habitually sought out horses that would win for him and often made mounts that wouldn't win for anyone else do so for him surely indicates his desire and need for success. He

Archer posing for the camera in his conservatory at Falmouth House. (Courtesy of the National Horseracing Museum, Newmarket)

hated failure. It was his nature to go out and win at all costs, even when, as was often the case, he had his own money on another horse in the race. The accusations that began to fly at the courses and in the press after he had ridden a bad race or not won when he was expected to do so bit deeply into Archer's mental state. He was the toast of the crowd when he had brought a horse home first, but then the self-same audience would turn against him if he was beaten and they would turn to scurrilous claims of cheating to explain their failure to back the winner.

On 31 January 1883 at the Church of All Saints in Newmarket, Fred Archer took Helen Rose Dawson as his wife. It was the social occasion of the year and widely written about. Presents came from all quarters of society and the couple enjoyed a short honeymoon in Torquay before Fred returned to the racetrack. It was to be a short and tragic marriage. On 10 January the following year Helen gave birth to a son, William, who died after a few hours. She remained ill and weak for a good while afterwards, but was soon expecting another baby. That baby, a girl called Nellie Rose, arrived on 7 November of the same year, but the ordeal proved too much for Helen's constitution and she died just hours afterwards. Fred was inconsolable. His dreams were suddenly turned on their head, all ambitions went out of the window and all reason for living had died with his wife.

The wedding of Fred Archer to Helen Rose Dawson, 31 January 1883. (Courtesy of The National Horseracing Museum, Newmarket)

His friends and family feared so much for him that they undertook to send him away to take his mind off the tragic events. On 15 November 1884 Fred Archer left for a four-month trip to America with his friend Captain Bowling and his valet William Bartholomew. Before setting out he returned to Cheltenham to have his solicitor, Jessop, write up his will. His fame was such at this time that it had extended over the Atlantic and he was fêted almost wherever he went. He toured the length of the country visiting Texas, Florida, Washington, Chicago, even venturing to Montreal in Canada, but it was strictly a tourist trip and when offered a sum of £2,000 to ride one race in the New World he politely declined.

When he eventually returned to England he took the racing world once more by storm. It was the year that he set that record of 246 winners and he won all the Classics save the 1000 Guineas. Mat Dawson had in his yard at that time two outstanding colts named Melton and Paradox which Archer largely managed to keep in separate races and ride both to success. With Paradox he took the 2000 Guineas and the Champion Stakes as well as the Grand Prix de Paris; then Archer chose Melton above Paradox for the Derby and duly won by a head from the horse that he had dropped. The year 1885 was also when he started bringing the Duke of Westminster's horse Ormonde home in the major races; the Criterion Stakes, Gimcrack Stakes and Dewhurst Plate were all theirs and significant indicators of the form of this wonderful horse. For all this success, however, Archer was still mourning the loss of his wife and little happiness was brought by his achievements. He was throwing himself into his work to stop the pain and he was inevitably working himself into the grave. The years of wasting, the constant toil to be the best, the tragedies that had occurred and the accusations that intermittently reappeared were working like a cancer in Archer.

On 27 May 1886 Archer won his fifth Derby, this time on Ormonde, and on the same horse took the St Leger – the final classic that Archer would win and on a horse that Archer believed could have been ridden by anyone and still come back a winner – but he was deeply conscious that he was not riding at his best. Still, Archer was pushing for victories and in October 1886 he paid his visit to the Curragh where he rode for Lord Londonderry and then picked up another mount called Isidore. He was wasting continually to make the weights and returned to England on a mail boat in order to be back in time for the Cambridgeshire Stakes for which he had been booked to ride St Mirin for the Duchess of Montrose. He lost that race by the smallest of margins to a rank outsider called Sailor Prince, and immediately rumours were rife that he had thrown the race. On the Friday following he rode his last ever winner. It was the last race of the day on a horse called Blanchard and fittingly enough he was wearing the magpie colours of Lord Falmouth, for it was one of the very few horses Falmouth still had in training.

Archer on Ormonde, painted by Alfred Wheeler. (Courtesy of the National Horseracing Museum, Newmarket)

Fred Archer with his daughter Nellie Rose shortly before his death. (Courtesy of The National Horseracing Museum, Newmarket)

Fred Archer's grave in Newmarket cemetery where he lies with his wife and infant son.

On 4 November 1886 he rode his last race, at Lewes, on Tommy Tittlemouse, an odds-on favourite that he couldn't get into the placings. He was clearly an ill man and returned to Newmarket to take to his bed. The following morning his doctor diagnosed that he had a high fever and severe chill. On 8 November, having consulted with another doctor who had arrived to give a second opinion on the great jockey's state of health, a diagnosis of typhoid fever was given. He was in a state of delirium and depression. Around two o' clock he asked his sister, Emily Coleman, who was at his bedside, to send the nurse away as he had something private to say to her. She did so and momentarily looked away, waiting for her brother to speak. Suddenly Fred was half out of bed with a revolver in his hand (this was kept in his bedside cabinet in case of burglars). She fought to grab the gun from him, but he managed to get it to his head and pulled the trigger. At 2.25 p.m. Fred Archer, thirteen times champion jockey, lay dead by his own hand in the home that he had built for his wife and family.

Fred Archer's ghost riding across Newmarket Heath, painted by Alfred Tilt in 1887. The inscription beneath the picture is as follows:

Across the heath – along the course
'Tis said that now on phantom horse
The greatest horse jockey of our days
Rides nightly in the moonlight rays.

(Courtesy of The National Horseracing Museum, Newmarket)

Public mourning was immediate and unrestrained, and late editions of the papers were published to carry the news. In next to no time memorial souvenirs were to be found everywhere. When he was buried on 12 November in Newmarket cemetery beside his wife and son mourners attended from all over Britain, France and Ireland, wreaths were sent by all ranks of society and the funeral was conducted by his friend John Baghot de la Bere, once rector of Prestbury and a member of that famous Prestbury family.

When his will was proved in January of the following year it was seen that the uneducated boy from Prestbury had left an estate valued at £60,000. His daughter, Nellie Rose, was brought up by Mat Dawson's daughter Annie in Newmarket and later when they moved in Marlow. Thirty-nine years after his death the name of Fred Archer was once again winning races, this time in National Hunt. The nephew of the great flat race jockey, working from Newmarket, trained Double Chance to win the Grand National, beating Old Tay Bridge by four lengths.

2

Billy Speck

Living in the village of Bishops Cleeve, William James Speck and William George Stott were largely referred to as the 'Two Billys'. They were great friends and regularly socialised together, and although it is Billy Stott that has the historical recognition of great riding achievements, those that saw Billy Speck ride rated him among the best jockeys of his genre, as good some said as the great Dick Rees. The lives of the two Billys were remarkably entwined, from the homes that they lived in, to the occupation that they both mastered, to their tragic untimely deaths.

Billy Speck was born in Lewes, Sussex, and at the tender age of just eleven was apprenticed to trainer Harry Escott, following in the footsteps of his father who rode some winners for Lewes trainers. When Escott couldn't give the young jockey enough opportunities he moved to the stables of Dick Wootton in Epsom where he would meet and forge a friendship that would last his lifetime with Billy Stott. They were apprentices together and rode on the flat together, Speck clearly holding the upper hand throughout their flat racing careers. As an apprentice in 1919 Speck won seven of his races, one fewer than Stott in that year but he also managed a second placing in the 1919 Cesarewitch at Newmarket on Golden Melody, losing to Ivanhoe. The following year Billy Speck really showed his form and notched up 25 winners, then 18 in 1921. After that, however, he was suffering the same sort of fate as his friend, Stott; with the loss of his allowance and rising weight he was being offered fewer rides and was able to make less of an impact. In 1922 he was still given 73 mounts, but could only convert one of these into a victory, so he turned to National Hunt racing.

His first win under National Hunt rules came in September 1922 at Ross-on-Wye. It was an unimpressive race with Speck riding Lady Flare first past the post in a selling race worth just £58 to the victor, but it was the first in a career that would make him one of the most bankable jockeys of his age. He had impressed enough to be given 44 mounts in that first season under National Hunt rules, 6 of which he converted into winners. The following season he had 72 mounts and twice the number of winners as in the previous year. In 1924 he was consolidating his position as a jockey, taking 18 of his 125 mounts first past the winning post. Then by 1925 he had surely arrived. He was booked for 225 rides and converted 54 of them into winners, making him third placed in the jockeys' championship behind Dick Rees who had 73 winners and Eric Foster who had 76. For the following ten years he would never finish worse than third

The Barracks Handicap Steeplechase at Windsor with, left to right, Slater with Everett up, Shadow with Billy Speck and General Advance with Billy Stott.

in the jockeys' tally; he never won the title but was runner-up six times and it is worth noting that although Billy Stott won the title five times in succession, for the three years before he took his first title and for the three years following his last title, Billy Speck won more races than he did. Furthermore had his last season not been cut so tragically short, Billy Speck would surely have won more than the 45 winners that he did and thus elevated him above the fourth placing in the table of that year. His accumulated tally of winners would amount to 640.

In 1926 he was offered his first ride in the Cheltenham Gold Cup, on Mr C.H. Horrell's Postino. The two finished a creditable fourth with Speck's friend and fellow Bishops Cleeve inhabitant, Tim Hamey, winning on Koko. The following day he won the Cotswold Steeplechase at the Festival on Preface with Jack Anthony's mount Slieve Rue coming second and Drumhirk third. Later that year he was given his first ride on a horse that so impressed Speck that he would later name a house after it, Zeno. Their first race together was at Sandown on 3 December 1926 in a Three Year Old Hurdle Race which they won. On the 11th of the same month they went on to win the Ashdown Juvenile Hurdle Race at Lingfield and then the Headley Juvenile Race at Gatwick just five days later. Zeno's next race was on 15 January 1927 at Hurst Park in the Mortlake Handicap Hurdle Race, and it brought a momentary halt to the pair's winning ways – they fell. But after a race in which George Duller brought Zeno home third, Speck was reunited with the horse for the Imperial Cup at Sandown on 19 March. Carrying a weight of 10 stone 12 lb, horse and jockey stormed home eight lengths clear of George Duller on Tide to start an impressive record that Speck would hold in the race. A month later they were racing to victory again, this time at Manchester in the Jubilee Handicap Hurdle Race on 19 April. In just over five months Speck and Zeno had won an incredible five out of their six rides together. The following season would not see such great accomplishments, although they won the General Peace Open Hurdle Race at Lingfield on 10 February 1928, beating Ted Leader on Peace River in the process. They failed ever to win a race again together. Peace River and Leader turned the tables on them in March by winning the Lingfield Hurdle Cup and they came fourth in the Champion Hurdle when Brown Jack won it on 15 March. For the Imperial Cup Speck took the ride on Le Gros instead of Zeno. Speck came sixth, Zeno a disappointing ninth; the following year Speck was back with Zeno in the Imperial Cup but still only managed to finish fifth with George Duller winning on Hercules. Despite Zeno's failure to build on the impressive start to his career as a three- and four-year-old, he was one of the first of Speck's mounts with which he would be linked as the recognised rider and did much for the jockey's standing in the eyes of the public.

In 1927, the same year that Speck was riding so well with Zeno, he was again offered the ride on Postino in the Gold Cup held on 8 March. This time they finished out of the placings but Speck then went on to impress in the inaugural running of the Champion Hurdle held the day after by finishing second on Mr A.H. Tennent's Boddam. The race was of course won by the master hurdler George Duller on Blaris.

It would be a further six years before Speck would ride in the Gold Cup again. He was just over five foot in height, 'bandy as a coot' and an affable, generous man who made friends easily. He enjoyed a more than occasional drink after racing, but held a commitment that if he had imbibed he wouldn't race. Several times he had ridden his last booked ride, started a drink and then had to turn down a last minute ride due to another jockey being injured or the like. He was a man of principle and kept to it; not only did he know that if he rode having had a drink he would be putting himself in possible danger, but it was equally likely that he wouldn't be giving of his best.

Speck moved from Stockbridge to Bishops Cleeve when he married a local farmer's daughter called Lilian Webb, and built and moved into a bungalow opposite his in-laws' farm in Priory Lane. Here he would remain for several years, eventually moving to a house in Pittville that he would name after Thomond II, one of his best mounts, and then towards the end of his life to a house on the Old Bath Road he named after Zeno.

He would over the years have quite some success in the Imperial Cup. Notwithstanding his success with Zeno, in 1930 he finished third on Porthaon owned by Sir Malcolm McAlpine, behind two horses both owned by V. Emanuel, War Mist who was second and Rubicon II who was first, ridden by P. Donoghue.

The following year he finished second on Jugo to Georges Pellerin on Residue and on 23 March 1935 he partnered Negro to a short head victory in the race

The bungalow in Priory Lane, Bishops Cleeve, where Billy and Lilian Speck lived for the first few years of their married life.

from Fred Gurney on Shelly's Lane, Georges Pellerin on Henri's Choice a further two lengths behind. This would be the first of the horse's two successive wins in the race and followed a third place finish with Speck in the Liverpool Hurdle of the previous year when Advancer took the honours.

Throughout his career Billy Speck was given rides on many great horses. Apart from Negro and Zeno there was Knight Bachelor with whom he won the Spring Hurdle at Manchester on 1 April 1929, beating Billy Stott on Friarton in the process, then the very next day he partnered Windermere Laddie to win the Jubilee Handicap Hurdle Race at the same meeting. He also rode Avenger to win by eight lengths from twice Grand National winner Reynoldstown in the Lancashire Chase at Manchester on 2 April 1934, with Double Crossed he took the Stanley Chase at Liverpool on 22 March of the same year, and then with the same horse won the 1935 Champion Chase. At one time or another he was also booked to ride Mister Moon, Ponorogo, Wenceslaus, Dusty Foot and Donegal, but above all these horses it is his union with Thomond II that is best remembered.

By the 1933/4 season his mastery of the art of jockeying was never more obvious. He was consistently riding winners for Jack Anthony, for whom he was first jockey, and for many others who wished to book his services. However it was

The Old and Bold Cricket Team of 1933 who played behind the Crown and Harp pub in Bishops Cleeve. Seated in the front row, left to right: F. Minett, Major Ratcliffe, T. Harrison, J. (Tim) Hamey, G. Price. Standing: J. Aston, A. Taylor, M. Smith, R. Goring, W. (Billy) Speck, E. (Eddie) Driscoll and F. Lawrence.

the manner in which he controlled the small but free-spirited Thomond II from expending his strength and speed too soon in order for him to race for the finish with all guns blazing that was a great indicator of his ability in the saddle, especially when it is considered that Speck was little over five feet in height. In his genre it is widely held that there was no other jockey who could ride a horse into the last fence and home like Billy Speck; those rides on Thomond II indicated this more perhaps than any other and are along with his Imperial Cup rides his best epitaph.

Billy Speck won the Becher Chase at Liverpool on three occasions with Thomond II all in succession, the first being on 9 November 1932 in a race that firmly established the jockey's credentials. Before Thomond II and Speck had got to Becher's Brook, the horse's saddle had begun to slip. Having cleared the brook, Speck tried to adjust the saddle and in so doing put the horse off. As a consequence the horse made a bad mistake two jumps from home and very nearly came down on his knees. Speck kept control of his mount, kept him on his feet and then pushed the saddle behind him so that he was riding bareback. Clearing the final fence in such a fashion, his legs firmly gripping the horse's side, he drove for home. With the saddle and weight-cloths dangling underneath the

A day at Cheltenham's races. Left to right: Mrs Mundy, Billy Speck, Lilian Speck, Ivy Stott, Len Lefebve, Tim Hamey.

horse, Speck pushed him past the odds-on favourite Colliery Band ridden by Gerald Hardy to win by half a length. It was an outstanding display of riding.

For the 1933 Becher Chase they put on such a display of supremacy that they finished fifteen lengths clear of second-placed Gregalach, the horse that had won the Grand National in 1929 and then been runner-up in 1931. The following year they would make it three in a row by coming home three lengths clear of Drintyre.

Thomond II was without any doubt a top class steeplechaser. His misfortune was that he was racing during the same age as an even better steeplechaser, a horse that if not the best ever to have jumped fences in Britain is certainly the second best – Golden Miller.

On 25 November 1933 Golden Miller and Thomond II with Gerald Wilson and Billy Speck respectively fought out the Lingfield Open Steeplechase with the Miller taking the honours, Speck and his mount second and Kellsboro Jack and Dudley Williams third. Thomond II avenged this Lingfield defeat on faster ground at Kempton Park in the Gamecock Handicap Chase on Boxing Day. With 7 lb less weight than the Miller, Thomond II won a fast run race by two lengths. Thomond II was not then in the line up for the 1934 Gold Cup, as he was being saved for the Grand National, so Speck was given the ride on Royal Ransom – another of Jock Whitney's talented horses. At the end of the day none could master

Golden Miller who won his third successive title by six lengths and thus struck up a record that only he has gone on to beat. Royal Ransom came in fourth place.

For the Grand National, Golden Miller was going for the unprecedented double and Billy Speck had the ride on Thomond II to try and prevent him. Up to that point Billy Speck had an unimpressive record in the Grand National, as all the horses he had ridden he had either fallen from or had refused. Throughout the 1934 race Speck shadowed Gerald Wilson on Golden Miller while Delaneige made much of the running. At the final fence however Thomond II was beginning to weaken. Miller took over the lead from Delaneige and went on to win, Speck bringing his horse home five lengths behind Delaneige in third place.

Sadly the following season was to prove the last for Speck, but it was also surely his most exciting. He was clearly at the pinnacle of his riding ability and for a spell before Christmas 1934 he was winning with 50 per cent of his mounts – an incredible statistic in any racing era. He was still given the rides on Thomond II with whom he had had such success; this horse would surely have achieved even more had he not been fated to be racing in the same age as Golden Miller. On the odd occasions that Thomond II had finished in front of the Miller, it was never to secure a famous victory in a race that really mattered. The 1935 Gold Cup seemed the time when that situation could be corrected. Ultimately it failed to bring Speck and Thomond II the glory they so richly deserved, but it did produce a racing spectacle that has not been bettered in the race's history.

The Cheltenham Jockeys Cricket Team, c. 1934. Standing, left to right: ? Newall, W. White, G. Pullen, G.S. Wood, T.F. Rimell, F. Taylor. Seated: Umpire D.L. Jones, J.H. Hamey with Rex Hamey, W. Speck, G. Wilson with John Hamey, E. Foster, E. Driscoll.

The details of much of the race are related in the history of Gerald Wilson who rode the Miller in that glorious race, for as victor it is surely his story to be told. For Speck it was once again the situation of finishing second best. Leading up to the race it was expected and widely reported that he would ride Royal Ransom, who it will be remembered was also owned by Jock Whitney, with Thomond II again being saved for the Grand National. However, with twenty-four hours left before the race, trainer Jack Anthony received a telegram from Jock Whitney instructing him to declare Thomond II for the Gold Cup. The decision sent shock-waves through the Miller camp; when the news reached the press the interest it produced brought a public reaction not seen before at Cheltenham. The great showdown between Golden Miller and Thomond II was on the cards, with two great jockeys at the pinnacle of their profession in the saddles.

Later Speck confided to Gerry Wilson that there had always been the intention for Thomond II to race in the Gold Cup and that a smokescreen had been put up to suggest otherwise. The dry conditions were perfectly suited to the horse and knowing that Basil Briscoe wouldn't fully wind Golden Miller up for the race if Thomond II wasn't running, Billy Speck had been going to Wantage twice a week to ride the horse in his gallops, confident that they would be able to put one over on Dorothy Paget and her champion. Whether it was right or wrong for Whitney to put his prize horse into the Gold Cup instead of saving him for the Grand National will never be known. Doing so certainly created a very memorable race that is part of Cheltenham racing folklore. Speck had ridden a perfect race on the horse and it was only the Miller's greater equine ability that lost them the victory.

In typical sporting and gracious fashion Speck raised his glass of champagne to Wilson while in Sir John Grey's box after the race and declared, 'It was a grand race, mate. And don't forget, when we are old we can sit back in our chairs and tell them that we did ride at least one day in our lives!' – to the grief of so many Speck was never able to fulfil that prophecy of his.

For the horses it was in reality the last great moment in two great racing careers. Thomond II went with Speck to Liverpool for the Grand National, once again to pit his ability against the Miller's. At the first fence Thomond II was disputing the lead with Theras and was always in contention long after Golden Miller had left the race by unseating Gerald Wilson. At the final fence Speck was in competition with Frank Furlong on Reynoldstown for the lead, then gradually the strength began to sap from the courageous horse. Reynoldstown opened out a lead and in the final 200 yards Blue Prince with William Parvin passed Speck and Thomond II. Realising that his horse was spent and beaten Speck refused to punish the small horse and eased him to the post, finishing eleven lengths behind the winner.

Thomond II never won another race and Billy Speck rode his last race at Cheltenham in April of that year.

On Wednesday 10 April in the first race of the Cheltenham Spring Meeting, the Ledbury Handicap Steeplechase, Billy Speck was booked to ride the terrible Gwelo, from trainer Len Lefebve's Prestbury stables. One story narrates how Speck was actually booked to ride Rollanbutta, but owing to his friend Tim Hamey's rather poor recent run, swapped the ride with him to ride Gwelo. Also riding among the eight runners was fellow local Frenchie Nicholson on Beauté du Diable. The punters were so convinced of Speck and his mount's superiority in the race that they backed him down to 2/1 against. In reality they weren't backing the horse but the jockey, such was the regard in which he was held. In the weighing rooms his fellow jockeys were so surprised that Speck should opt to ride such a bad horse that some of them even told him to get off the mount.

It was almost inevitable that tragedy would strike. At the fence after the waterjump Speck was unseated from Gwelo and then didn't get up. Ignorant of the seriousness of the jockey's fall the riders naturally carried on, with second favourite Derelict taking the race and Tim Hamey on Rollanbutta coming in second. The racecourse ambulance was belatedly summoned and made its way to the stricken jockey. Soon it was realised that the injuries sustained by the little man were serious: it would later be ascertained that his spine had been broken. Immediately a flag was waved to get a doctor to the scene, but disgracefully the racing timetable was left unaffected and the jockey lay prone where he had fallen when they sent the second race off.

Eventually the racecourse ambulance brought him back to the grandstands where he was put into another and rushed to the Royal Nursing Home in Cheltenham. Six days later on 16 April, just before 5 p.m., Billy Speck gave up his brave fight for life. He was just thirty-one years of age, he had been riding for fifteen seasons and had ridden over 600 winners. His wife Lilian, son Victor William, and two daughters, Peggy (who later married George Slack) and Sybell,

Bishops Cleeve St Michael and All Angels' church. It is here that both Tim Hamey and Billy Speck are buried.

had lost a husband and father. The racing world had lost the jockey who was heralded as without a peer over hurdles since the retirement of George Duller and equal to the best over fences. Jack Moloney stated after his death that 'he was probably the greatest [jockey] in England'; Tim Hamey proclaimed him 'the best jockey riding today'.

On 19 April Billy Speck was laid to rest at Bishops Cleeve church. The funeral procession and public grieving was such that is rarely seen in Cheltenham. Over 2,000 people attended with hundreds following the cortège as it came from Cheltenham past Prestbury Park, the scene of so many of his triumphs and of his ultimate tragedy, where the flag flew at half-mast and on to Bishops Cleeve. They made the journey by car, bicycle, foot and specially booked buses to pay their last respects.

At the church Tim Hamey, Billy Stott, Len Lefebve, Ben Roberts, Eddie Driscoll and Jack Moloney

Billy Speck's grave in the Bishops Cleeve churchyard; note the interesting spelling of his 'nickname'.

served as pall-bearers. As the coffin was lowered in to the grave Len Lefebve threw in the jacket that the jockey had been wearing when he fell; his crop and saddle were already with him. The epitaph on the headstone reads:

> Life's race well run
> Life's work well done
> Then comes rest.

In years to come his son Vic married Peggy Roberts, sister to trainer John Roberts, and would follow his father's footsteps and ride successfully over jumps, but he never quite had the natural ability that Billy possessed, and later turned to training at Melton Mowbray. Victor Speck died in January 1989 at the age of sixty-three.

3

Billy Stott

Before the start of the 1933 Grand National, some critics of five-time champion jockey Billy Stott admired him for his superb jockeymanship over park courses but said that he was too short in the leg, too light and altogether the wrong type to successfully tackle the huge Aintree fences with their massive drops on the landing side. Because of this opinion he was dropped from riding Golden Miller in the race, with Ted Leader being given the ride instead. Incredibly this decision was after Stott had just won the Cheltenham Gold Cup on the Dorothy Paget-owned horse and must be seen as one of the most flawed decisions and criticisms to have been made at such a high level of racing. Understandably the brave little jockey, who had proved himself as one of the best of his day, was deflated. Among his many prizes the Grand National wasn't included and to be discarded from riding the best steeplechaser in England in the race was a tremendous blow.

Nevertheless, a jockey who had been at the top of his profession as long as Billy Stott had wasn't about to allow a little bit of opinion to upset him. He had previously been offered the ride on a horse called Pelorus Jack owned by Ben Davis, but turned it down as he felt sure that Paget and Briscoe would honour their agreement for him to partner Golden Miller. The Pelorus Jack offer hadn't been an empty one either, for Ben Davis reputedly offered him £250 to take the ride and ten times that amount if the horse won. Money was not Billy Stott's god, but when the ride on Golden Miller was taken away he naturally opted for Pelorus Jack and duly set about proving his critics wrong, and most specifically proving to Dorothy Paget and Basil Briscoe, Golden Miller's owner and trainer respectively, that whichever of them had believed him inadequate, if not both of them, was positively naïve and had misjudged him.

When Golden Miller unseated Ted Leader on the second circuit of the National and Billy Stott was later contesting the lead on Pelorus Jack with Dudley Williams on Kellsboro Jack, it seemed that an incredible turn of events was on the cards that would forever silence Stott's critics. It seemed that Stott was really going to rub salt in the wounds of the Miller's connections. Pelorus Jack was a giant of a horse, not widely fancied in the race and certainly not the kind of horse that the critics would choose for the diminutive 'short-legged' Stott. From the start, the huge beast ensured that Stott's ability as a jockey would be tested and consequently highlighted. He almost fell at the first fence, but Stott kept him up and using all of his energy and the incredible strength in his shoulders and arms encouraged him round the course, gradually working his way through to the leaders. As a gap began to build it looked as though the race was between the two Jacks, Pelorus and Kellsboro, and that Stott was really going to right all the wrongs that had been committed against him by his critics. Then, at the last fence, with the two horses jumping level and contesting every inch of the way, Pelorus Jack seemed to die on his feet, his strength almost completely gone. Devastatingly, Pelorus Jack made a mistake, just caught his hind legs on that last fence and came sprawling to the ground; Billy Stott went flying from the saddle and 'bounced along the ground like a nut in a shell'. After the race Billy Stott told Ben Davis that there was something wrong with the horse. Interestingly, when the horse later died an autopsy revealed that he had an enlarged heart.

Even though he had not won, Billy Stott had ridden such a masterly race and come so close that the decision to drop him from the Golden Miller ride was appreciated as naïve and impulsive. Unfortunately it would be the last great race of Billy Stott's impressive career, but it is fitting that when his ability was questioned he was able to answer his critics.

William George Stott, the son of a footman, was born in Ripon, North Yorkshire, on 1 December 1898. He took up an apprenticeship to be a jockey with Dick Wootton in Epsom when he was well into his teens, slightly later than is normal. Dick Wootton, the father of Stanley Wootton the more famous tutor of apprentices and Frank Wootton the champion flat-racing jockey 1909–12, was an Australian who had emigrated to England in 1907. Like his son, he was an excellent tutor and under his tutelage the young Billy Stott rode quite successfully on the flat. As an apprentice in 1919 he notched up eight wins; the following year it was just two; none in 1921 but then two more in 1922 from seventeen mounts. It was evident that with the loss of his allowance the rides had begun to dry up and he wasn't going to make a great career on the flat; this, combined with his rising weight, meant that he was compelled to turn to the National Hunt. Nevertheless it was Stott's valuable training on the flat that would reap him the great rewards he would find on racing's other stage.

While he was at the Wootton stables he met and formed a friendship that would remain until death parted them with that other great jockey of the interwar years, Billy Speck.

After his five-year apprenticeship was over he began to look further afield to find more rides. As a consequence he moved to Stockbridge to join the Atty Persse stables, but this move did not result in a huge number of extra rides so he moved on to a stables in Devizes where the trainer went through such a bad patch that Stott had to help out periodically with the lads' wages. That trainer eventually closed down. A little later he took up rooms with farmer Jack Denley in Gambles Lane, Woodmancote, near Cheltenham, and held a position at Alf Newey's stables in New Road between Southam and Woodmancote. Newey was the winning jockey of the 1907 Grand National with the Couthwaite-trained Eremon, as well as being a runner-up in 1915 and third in 1905. It was from here that Stott's National Hunt career really took off.

The wedding of William George Stott to Ivy May Fisher at Christ Church, Epsom, 3 June 1922. This photograph was taken in Jack Oakshott's field, Lewins Road, Epsom.

With his rising weight, Stott turned to National Hunt racing in 1922, the same year that on 3 June he married Ivy May Fisher at Christ Church in Epsom. She was just nineteen years of age; he was twenty-three and on the verge of carving out a great racing career.

Later he would live for several years at Tuskar House (named after his winning mount in the Lancashire Chase) on the Cheltenham Road in Bishops Cleeve, near his friend Billy Speck and on the same stretch of road where his other contemporary Tim Hamey would be living.

He was given his first Grand National ride in 1926, the year of Jack Horner's three-length win over Old Tay Bridge, but as would be the trend with his appearances in this particular race, his horse, Lee Bridge, was a faller.

The season before his first championship season, the young Billy Stott was involved in one of the most controversial betting coups in National Hunt racing. It was in January 1927 at Tenby that the race occurred, and such was the devastation of the coup that it has singlehandedly been blamed for destroying National Hunt racing at many smaller racecourses and for most of Welsh racing. The race involved was the Licenced Victuallers Selling Handicap Hurdle Race over two miles, with prize money of only £50. There were just eight runners. It is not known who exactly was behind the coup, but there were plenty in the know who gave the bookies a real caning. The favourite was a horse named Bubbly ridden by the master jockey Dick Rees, who was going out at odds of 5/2. The four-year-old mare Oyster Maid, which was Billy Stott's mount, was given a

Tuskar House, Billy Stott's home in 'Jockeys' Row', Cheltenham Road, Bishops Cleeve.

starting price of 8/1, and it was around this horse that the coup was centred. The official starting price reporter and the jockeys were all apparently promised starting price odds to £50 for Oyster Maid should she win.

The weather was atrocious and the race was held in a veritable snowstorm. Any Excuse made the early running from Fairy Light, but then when the horses were out of view, the two amateur jockeys were impeded and the rest of the horses slowed to allow Bubbly and Oyster Maid to contest the finish. At the final flight Billy Stott pushed the mare ahead of Bubbly and won by an easy five lengths.

The bookmakers were completely roasted, with many large bets landing on the horse from all over the country just before the off. Billy Stott rode as a professional, going out and winning a race as per the norm; those in the background engineered a huge coup that rumour has it involved racecourse officials, jockeys, trainers and owners.

The following season, 1927/8, riding 88 winners – one of which was Tuskar in the Lancashire Chase at Manchester on 9 April 1928, a six-length winner from Low Tide – from 372 mounts, Billy Stott took the Champion National Hunt Jockey title for the first time. He took it from the five-time holder Dick Rees, regarded by many as the best National Hunt Jockey ever who won all of the classic races: the Grand National, the Cheltenham Gold Cup, the Champion Hurdle and the Grand Steeplechase de Paris. Stott himself wouldn't relinquish the title until he had gone on to win it five times in succession.

It is now customary for champion jockeys to be given a dinner in their honour at Cheltenham, paid for by the Cheltenham Steeplechase Company. Today these dinners are appropriately held at the racecourse itself but have in the past been held at the now lost Plough Hotel in Cheltenham and the Queen's Hotel. When Billy Stott won the championship in the 1929/30 season it was he who footed the bill for the entire meal given at the Queen's Hotel on 12 November 1930, an act of generosity that was typical of the man. There was no expense spared, with cigars, 1875 Courvoisier brandy, port and 1923 Heidsieck champagne all being offered to his guests along with the meal.

A sociable, talkative and amiable man, but also rather reserved, Billy Stott was widely liked but, unlike many, didn't crave attention or glory. He chain-smoked, but unlike his greatest friend Billy Speck was a teetotaller, save for the occasional port and lemon at Christmas. He was famous for drinking nothing but tea. Even though his talent as a jockey would be acclaimed and his strength and courage respected, he would avoid getting on a horse if at all possible outside racing. His courage was such that by the end of his career it was suggested in the press that the jockey who was just 5 foot tall and never weighed more than 9 stone had broken nearly every bone in his body, and those that he hadn't broken were not worth breaking. There was even one occasion when he broke his collar bone at a race meeting and then went on to win two more races on the same card!

A favourite mount was named Holiday Hall, a consistent but moderate chaser with whom he won a race towards the end of 1929 when he had an injured wrist. A little later he rode him at Chelmsford when the right rein broke during the early part of the race; he leaned up the neck and grabbed the remaining 18 inches of rein and in such a position rode the remaining two miles of the race. At the start of the straight he was lying in last place, at the finishing post he was three lengths clear of the field.

The following season, 1928/9, he rode 65 winners to clinch the title and rode in his first of three Cheltenham Gold Cups when he took Mr F.H.W. Cundell's Knight of the Wilderness into fourth place, and on the same day finished second to Royal Falcon in the Champion Hurdle on the Tom Rimell-trained Rolie. Two years later, and again ridden by Stott, this horse would beat Gerald Wilson on Golden Miller in the Spring Steeplechase at Newbury, and had in 1927 given Fred Rimell his first career win in a race at Chepstow. In the Grand National of that year he achieved what would be his best result in the race by riding Mr R. McAlpine's Richmond II into third place.

Stott would have to wait until 1932 before he rode in the Gold Cup again, but in between times he consolidated his position as champion jockey, riding 77 winners in 1929–30, among which was Glenhazel in the Lancashire Hurdle at Liverpool, and 81 winners in 1930–31.

For the 1932 Cheltenham Gold Cup he was on the disappointing Kingsford who fell, but once again he finished the season as champion for a fifth consecutive time, the first to achieve this and since equalled only by John Francome and bettered only by Gerald Wilson and Peter Scudamore. In that, the last season in which he took the champion jockey title, he finished with 77 winners; in second place in the table was Gerald Hardy on 69 winners, and with one winner less in

The menus of two of the Champion Jockey Dinners held at the Queens Hotel in Cheltenham for Billy Stott. Note that the one for the 1929/30 season was given by the man himself.

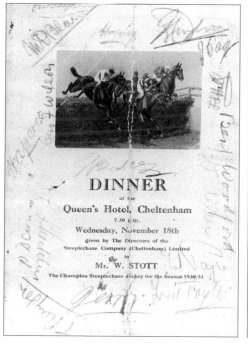

The 1929 Champion Hurdle with Royal Falcon jumping ahead to win with Dick Rees. Behind is Billy Stott on Rolie who lost the race by four lengths.

third place was Stott's great friend Billy Speck. Three of those 77 winners all came on 23 April 1932 at Sandown in successive races; the first race of that day was the St James Selling Handicap Hurdle Race which he won on Spectroscope, then with Cheviotdale he won the Pavilion Selling Handicap Steeplechase and in the Grand International Handicap Steeplechase he won with Cathalan.

The National of 1932 saw Stott on Lord Glenapp's Annandale who fell but, in typical never-say-die fashion, Stott remounted the horse and finished the course in sixth place, well behind the winning pair of Tim Hamey and Forbra, but still in front of the only other two finishers. Although he would end up losing the champion jockey title in 1932/3 to Gerald Wilson, it was the season for which he is perhaps best remembered for a whole catalogue of reasons, and had he not been so crippled by injuries at the end it is unlikely that Wilson would have wrenched the title away from him.

On 1 March he was partnered with Forbra, the previous year's Grand National winner, trained by Tom Rimell at Kinnersley, to win the Coventry Trial Handicap Steeplechase and then a week to the day later he was booked to ride the best hurdler in the country at that time, Insurance, for Dorothy Paget in the Champion Hurdle at Cheltenham. Insurance had been bought at the same time as Golden Miller by Dorothy Paget when the ailing Philip Carr decided to sell his collection of racehorses. The pair of horses were supposedly bought for the total

The Lingfield Open Chase on 10 December 1932. Tim Hamey leads on Gib with W. Ransom in second on Huic Holloa and Billy Stott in third on Golden Miller. The Miller eventually won by three lengths from Huic Holloa, with Gib trailing in a bad third.

sum of £12,000. Basil Briscoe, their trainer both before and after the change in ownership, was firmly of the opinion that she was buying the best steeplechaser and the best hurdler in the country. How right he was. Golden Miller's success is now well chronicled, and Insurance won the 1932 Champion Hurdle with Ted Leader, and Stott guided him to success in the Sefton Steeplechase at Newbury on 20 January 1933, when they beat Gerald Hardy on Ready Cash by a short head with Gerry Wilson on Via Fitzroi a further three lengths behind. Stott was then asked to ride the Champion Hurdler at Cheltenham to defend his title.

On Tuesday 8 March 1933 the public clearly thought that Insurance would win again as he went off odds-on favourite at 10/11. However, at the start Stott was attacked by the previous year's runner-up, Song of Essex, who grabbed and savaged his arm. The start of the race was delayed a few minutes but resolute and determined, Stott wrapped a handkerchief around the wound and declared himself ready to ride. The ground was heavy from recent rain and the five horses set a slow pace. Coming down the hill, Stott took control of the inside rail and passed Tees Head. At the last hurdle he pushed the six-year-old Insurance to the limit. They won by three quarters of a length from Staff Ingham on Windermere Laddie, Indian Salmon finishing in third place a further eight lengths behind. With barely time to draw breath Stott left the winning enclosure, got a little medical attention for his arm and went to mount Dorothy Paget's other great horse, Golden Miller, who was to ride in the very next race, the Gold Cup, which he was defending for the first time.

Stott had first ridden the great horse at Chelmsford on Monday 12 October 1931 in the Witham Hurdle Race which they won by ten lengths. For the remainder of that season the Miller was ridden by Ted Leader with whom he had won the 1931 Gold Cup, save for an amateur riders' Hurdle Race at Manchester

Five-time champion Jockey Billy Stott.

at the end of October, but by the time of the 1933 National Hunt Festival Stott had had all the rides on Golden Miller for that season, starting at Kempton Park on 1 December 1932 when they won a two-and-a-half mile steeple-chase. After that they went for three-mile steeplechases and proved themselves invulnerable. Going to the post the Miller was odds-on favourite at 4/7; second favourite was the seven-year-old Thomond II at 11/4 who was ridden by Billy Speck. Also in the race were Kellsboro Jack, Delaneige, the Brown Talisman, Holmes and Inverse. As with the previous race, the going was heavy, but Golden Miller was in a different class from the other runners. Third fence from last Stott and his mount jumped clear of Speck and Thomond II and then just kept on opening up space. At the post Golden Miller was ten lengths clear from Thomond II with Delaneige a further three lengths behind. The horse hadn't been extended.

From the beginning of the season it had been the aim of Dorothy Paget and Basil Briscoe for Golden Miller to win the Grand National, and following the horse's total annihilation of the other Gold Cup runners there was considerable confidence in the horse's camp that he would do just that. It must have been disappointing to say the least for Billy Stott to learn that he wouldn't get the ride in the race that really mattered. Despite the fact that in his six rides on Miller they had been unbeaten, Briscoe and Paget were swayed perhaps by the press, perhaps because they didn't feel that he had the necessary experience of Aintree. Whatever the reason they were proved wrong in their assessment of Billy Stott and almost had their noses rubbed in it. Instead the ride returned to Ted Leader who had ridden him with mixed success the previous season (together they had won four out of eight races). Billy Stott never rode the Miller again and incidentally never rode again in the Gold Cup.

Days after almost winning the Grand National, Billy Stott was returning home to Bishops Cleeve from a day's racing at Epsom, when passing Dowdeswell reservoir, just on the eastern perimeter of Cheltenham, he had to brake suddenly and swerve to avoid hitting a man on foot. He was driving his wife's Morris Cowley and it overturned, resulting in him being pinned beneath it. Fortunately a passing motorist stopped and rescued him and rushed him to Cheltenham

Billy Stott up on the Tom Rimell-trained Tide at Newbury.

General Hospital. Stott's injuries were found to be a broken nose, a fractured jawbone and serious damage to the bone over his right eye. The accident occurred in April 1933 and Stott was not allowed back into racing until October of that year, having had to undergo plastic surgery to rebuild parts of his injured face.

His first race back was on Pelorus Jack, that massive horse that had so nearly won the National. At the last fence the horse crumpled and Billy Stott was once again thrown out of the saddle and put back to bed. Almost immediately he developed pneumonia that racked his constitution and had people saying that he was past racing.

Billy Stott being led out at Ludlow.

The small but iron-willed jockey wouldn't give up easily and in November he was back in the saddle, but a mere two days later he was again injured and laid up. Again there were those who said he wouldn't or couldn't return. Proving them wrong he came back once again and finished the year with three winners at Wolverhampton on 27 December: Wardlow in the Compton Selling Hurdle Race, Gillgowan in the Open Three Year Old Hurdle Race and Donnybrook in the Stanton Selling Handicap Chase. Then on 8 January 1934 he had a double at Leicester: Pure Food in the Hinckley Handicap Hurdle Race, which beat Fulke Walwyn's mount Chacrero by four lengths and in the following race, the Stayer's Handicap Hurdle Race, he partnered Landseer to a one-and-a-half length victory over Lord Nugent ridden by Mr Payne-Gallwey. By the end of the season he had still managed to notch up 21 victories from 124 rides.

Despite his amazing willpower, it was clear even to himself that he couldn't continue racing forever, especially after a career that had seen him suffer so much injury. So he bought in partnership with his father-in-law a laundry business in Epsom, where he moved from Bishops Cleeve. The laundry business used in its advertising the rather novel slogan: 'Instead of putting your shirt on Billy Stott put it in his laundry.'

For a short while he continued to race with gradually decreasing success. His critics said that his eyesight was shot and that his nerve was failing. In typical fashion he responded by offering to ride in two races at any course with his left and right eyes alternately bandaged. This silenced both accusations.

In 1935, the year in which his heart was broken by the sudden death of his great friend Billy Speck who died in the April, Billy Stott retired from racing, having ridden just four winners in the 1934/5 season. He took more interest in his business and indulged more in his hobby of dog racing, having a particularly good dog by the name of Bamford Castle who won a number of races.

Early on the Sunday morning of 11 October 1936, at the tender age of thirty-seven, Billy Stott died from a massive heart attack at his Epsom home. He left behind a wife and two young sons, Bill and Roy. It was just eighteen months after the death of Billy Speck. The two jockeys who had been so much akin in life had both died when only in their thirties.

The five-time champion jockey, winner of both the Gold Cup and the Champion Hurdle, and the rider of more than 600 winners, was mourned throughout the racing world, not just for his accomplishments in the saddle

Billy Stott up on Tuskar. This favoured mount of Stott's was killed while being shipped to France when he was frightened by the siren going off and hit his head.

but also for his generosity and affability. At 2 o'clock on the day that his funeral was taking place at Christ Church in Epsom a bookmaker at Newmarket mounted a form in the Tattersall's ring and gravely said 'Gentlemen'. It was the signal for a minute's silence adhered to respectfully in the rings, the stands, by the jockeys in the weighing room and the public all along the course.

4

Gerry Wilson

On 15 March 1935 arguably the best Cheltenham Gold Cup to date was run. The three-time Gold Cup winner Golden Miller faced Thomond II, a horse of outstanding ability who would have achieved far more if he hadn't been fated to live in the same era as the Miller. The two horses were old adversaries with the Miller holding the upper hand. When Dorothy Paget's horse won his second Gold Cup in 1933, Thomond II trailed in ten lengths behind in second place; in the 1934 Grand National which Golden Miller won to achieve the incredible double of Gold Cup and National in the same year, Thomond II finished third.

When the two faced each other in the 1935 Gold Cup however, the conditions were much more suited to Thomond II. An extremely dry spring had produced very hard ground which was better going for Thomond than the Miller, the Miller's jockey was unfit and the horse itself was not run in fully. Furthermore, Billy Speck, Thomond II's jockey, was at the pinnacle of his career. The stage was set for Golden Miller to be defeated.

Golden Miller went to post odds-on favourite at 1/2, and Thomond II was second favourite at 5/2. It was a match that Basil Briscoe, Golden Miller's trainer, hadn't expected. Twenty-four hours before the race only Kellsboro Jack, Southern Hero and Avenger were due to race against his horse and the race was marked as a warm-up gallop for Golden Miller's assault on the Grand National on 29 March. But Thomond II's American owner J.H. 'Jock' Whitney wanted to see him race in the Gold Cup; he made his other horse, Royal Ransom, till then a possible runner in the race, a non-runner, and installed Thomond II. Golden Miller's connections were horrified, as a hard race in the Gold Cup could severely affect his run in the National.

There was more to worry about as the jockey booked for the Miller ride was injured; he had fallen in the National Trial Steeplechase on 2 March 1935 at Gatwick from a horse called D'Eyncourt trained by Frank Brown and had badly torn his shoulder muscles. Consequently he hadn't taken another ride in public until Shirley Park on the Monday of Festival Week to see if his shoulder would stand the strain. That day he had three mounts, Ghazala in the Brook Hurdle (unplaced), Genius in the Hall Green Selling Handicap Hurdle Race (finished second) and The Smiler who came third in the Olton Handicap Hurdle Race. The next day he rode Lion Courage in the Champion Hurdle on the first day of the Cheltenham Festival for the Bourton-on-the-Hill trainer Frank Brown. Lion Courage, who had taken the Imperial Cup the previous year with the same jockey, came home first in record time beating Gay Light into second and Hill Song into third. However on unsaddling the jockey found that he couldn't lift his left arm to undo the girths; there was no pain, it was just weak and useless. He then decided to announce that he wouldn't take any other rides save Golden Miller in the Gold Cup – a race that at that time he was also convinced would be just a gentle gallop for the great horse – and left for London to have some electric treatment on the arm to bring the strength back.

With the late announcement that Thomond II was going to run against Golden Miller, a frenzy of public interest in the race was aroused. Extra trains had to be put on for Cheltenham and the roads all around the town became crammed.

The race was no anti-climax. Southern Hero set the running and all the horses jumped with precision. Third from last, Golden Miller and Thomond II closed on the leader and then overtook him in mid air over the fence. The speed that they were running had not been seen in the race before and there was nothing between the two horses as they careered over the last two fences, each being ridden for all their worth. As they stormed up the hill, the strength of the mighty Golden Miller just began to show, but Thomond II refused to give way; he fought all the way to the finish, but the Miller was just too strong and he won by three-quarters of a length.

Ultimately the race exacted its price as Thomond II finished a distant third in the National and Golden Miller unseated his rider: the same rider who had

The very young Gerald Wilson on what was possibly his first pony.

guided the horse home when in such considerable pain from his shoulder; the rider who had won the Gold Cup the previous year with Golden Miller and was in fact champion jockey, a title that he would claim on seven occasions and the rider who had done the 'double' with the Miller the previous year when they won the National; the rider who, when he turned his attention to training, would train the winner of the Champion Hurdle. The rider was Gerald Wilson.

The son of a horse dealer and colt breaker, Gerald Wilson was born on 12 October 1903 at Wing, near Leighton Buzzard, in the Whaddon Chase area. With horses all around him and his father a keen huntsman it was only natural that he learnt how to ride and master a horse early in life. In March 1915 he was sent to Frank Hartigan at Weyhill to become an apprentice jockey, but the stay was short-lived as after a few weeks he suffered an acute appendicitis resulting in him spending four months in hospital and having three operations. He was sent home in the summer to convalesce and didn't return to Weyhill to continue his apprenticeship until March of the following year. Racing was being severely affected by the war raging in Europe, but somehow meetings did take place, albeit on a limited scale, and Gerald Wilson got his first public mounts. It was soon apparent that he was going to be too big to ride on the flat for long so his mind began to turn to riding over jumps, a sport even more limited during the war than flat racing.

He finished his apprenticeship and returned home in early 1919. Some flat pony racing, showjumping, gymkhanas and hunting were his life, then later in that first year home he rode in his first steeplechase at Banbury, in a Novices' Steeplechase, on a horse co-owned by his father and a Mr Ralph Clarke. His first winner under National Hunt rules was not until Saturday 15 October 1921 when he rode Abbott's Wood in the three-mile Waterloo Steeplechase at Huntingdon – his only winner of the season, but having only four mounts a respectable tally!

For a while after leaving home he dabbled between racing, becoming a nagsman for a Mr Goodchild who bought horses to send to America and for a winter he privately schooled the racehorses of Captain Sassoon at Ogbourne with Teddie Martin. Then he felt the urge to rekindle his racing career, and so he contacted a trainer for whom he had had some successes while he was still living at home in Wing. The trainer was named Joseph Lovedren 'Sonny' Hall and he immediately agreed to take Gerry on to work and ride for him from his stables at Fenny Compton, Warwickshire.

Within two weeks of taking up the position Gerry had ridden a winner, Sorrel Hill, for his new stables in a race at Aylesbury, and then a week later on the Easter Monday he took the Towcester Open Steeplechase on Indian Mat. While at Fenny Compton Gerald Wilson won several races with a horse owned by Anthony Bellville named Roman Hackle. Anthony Bellville in later years then named another of his horses Roman Hackle, and it was this horse that went on to be sold to Dorothy Paget and trained by Owen Anthony, for whom he would win the 1940 Gold Cup.

As Wilson developed as a jockey it became apparent that he was naturally strong, very competitive and a courageous rider. He was also very intelligent. He studied horses meticulously and would always look for the best route round a course: often it would appear that he was taking the longest route, but then due to the going it would be seen that he was actually taking the shortest. Fred Rimell later admitted that he would often follow Wilson in a race, knowing full well that his brother-in-law was taking the best course. He was by no means an extrovert and kept himself to himself; indeed his own family nicknamed him 'Oyster' as he so rarely came out of his shell.

He rode in his first Grand National in 1929, the year of Gregalach, when sixty-six runners started the race. Wilson was on Delarue, trained by George Beeby at Waltham-on-the Wold. At the third fence he was stopped by Skrun Prince who refused, but Wilson turned his mount around and they finished a very creditable eighth from ten finishers. The following year Wilson was again given the ride on Delarue in the Grand National, and he experienced what he would later say was the only time that he felt really frightened during his racing career. At the open ditch after Valentine's on the first circuit, KCB, owned by Lord Bicester and being ridden by Jack Molony, refused and baulked. Wilson and Delarue were right with them and both horses fell into the ditch with their respective jockeys between them. They then had to sit tight as about thirty more horses thundered over them. Had there been another faller it could have been very nasty. When the two jockeys finally managed to escape from the ditch they found themselves covered in gorse prickles; they hadn't felt a thing while the hooves and bellies of the racehorses had been leaping over their heads!

The first big race that Wilson won was the Champion Chase at the Liverpool Spring Meeting with a little-known French horse, Coup de Chapeau, who was trained at Lewes by Eric Stedall and owned by American J. Drake, on Saturday 28 March 1931. Among the adversaries in the race was the mighty, albeit ageing, dual Gold Cup winner, Easter Hero, ridden by Dick Rees, who had ridden the previous day in the National, falling at Becher's second time around. At 12 stone level weights the race was a dead heat, and it was only the skill of Rees that enabled him to not be beaten by this unknown horse and its young jockey.

Earlier in the same year the young Wilson was asked by Basil Briscoe to come to his training stables at Longstowe near Cambridge to school a young horse of his over fences. As it happened Wilson knew the horse because on 26 January of that year he had finished second to him in the Annesley Hurdle Race at Nottingham riding Oliver Cromwell, Ted Leader being on the winner. The jockey took up the offer and was impressed by the strong devil of a horse, but not as much as the trainer, who believed that he was going to be the best horse ever seen. As a consequence of the schooling, Gerry Wilson was then offered the ride on the horse's first race over fences. The horse was named Golden Miller, and he would go on to prove all of Basil Briscoe's prophecies about him as being correct. That first National Hunt race was the Spring Steeplechase at Newbury on 21 February 1931. It was a very close-run contest with champion jockey Billy Stott winning by a head on Tom Rimell's Rolie.

On finishing the race Gerald Wilson informed Basil Briscoe and Philip W. Carr, the horse's owner at that time (and father of A.W. Carr, the Nottinghamshire cricketer who captained England against the Australians), that the horse was jumping across the fences and that he had to hit him on the side of his head to keep him going straight – idiosyncrasies of which the horse would never be fully cured.

It would be over two years before Wilson would sit astride the great horse again, but in the years to come he would be the jockey most often matched with Golden Miller; of the seventeen jockeys to ride him, Wilson rode him the most, fourteen times in total.

In the first season that he was crowned champion jockey, 1932/3, Gerry Wilson rode 61 winners. The following season he would become Champion again, although with a tally of winners five short of the previous year. However, in that second championship year he rode Golden Miller to the 'double', the Gold Cup and Grand National in the same season, the only horse to have achieved this feat to date.

With Ted Leader, Golden Miller had won his first Gold Cup in 1932. The following year it was with Billy Stott that he took the cup. But then the ever-changeable Dorothy Paget, who had bought Golden Miller in the winter of 1941 when P.W. Carr was ill and close to death, decided on yet another change of jockey and the champion jockey, Wilson, was marked as the horse's jockey for the 1934 Gold Cup and Grand National, with the Grand National being the principal aim. The lead-up to that finale started when during the summer of 1933 Wilson found himself at Newmarket, where he met Basil Briscoe. The trainer asked him to come and see Golden Miller, who was turned out for the summer. The horse was fat and out of shape, but Wilson was delighted when Briscoe asked him if he would come and school him. Then he was offered and accepted the ride at Lingfield Park on 25 November 1933 in the Lingfield Open Steeplechase. The going was very heavy, and the last words of the trainer to Wilson were 'For God's sake keep him straight over the last three or four fences, Gerry'. The jockey managed to keep him fairly straight, although Golden Miller began to hang badly to the right down the hill and going into the last three fences he had to hit him on the shoulder and cheek to keep him from running right across his fences. Wilson brought Golden Miller home a winner from Billy Speck on Thomond II and Dudley Williams on Kellsboro Jack. It was a memorable day all round for Wilson, for he had completed an incredible five wins out of five rides for the Lingfield meeting. On the previous day he won on his only mount, a horse called Courtesy in the Cowden Selling Steeplechase, then on the second day of the meeting along with Golden Miller he won on Dorothy Paget's Mr Punch II in the St Piers Selling Handicap Steeplechase, Wing Commander Read's Corkaree in the Winter Handicap Hurdle Race and the Frank Hartigan-trained The Spider in the Dormans Steeplechase. Golden Miller, Corkaree and The Spider won in successive races.

Golden Miller was not a fast horse over a short distance, but once he got going he had a killing stride and incredible endurance. A month later at Kempton Park, on Boxing Day, The Miller and Gerry Wilson had a reversal when they lost to Billy Speck and Thomond II in the Gamecock Handicap Steeplechase in a fast paced race over fast ground. Thomond II was receiving 7 lb and jumped superbly. Golden Miller tried hard to jump to the right over the last two fences, and Wilson couldn't quite get him on terms with the eventual victor.

The Star and Garter Handicap Steeplechase at Hurst Park was chosen as the final warm-up race for Golden Miller before the Gold Cup on 7 March. Giving 2 stone away to Southern Hero ridden by Jack Fawcus and owned by J.V. Rank, Golden Miller was being asked a near impossible task and Gerry Wilson pulled him up after jumping the last fence when in third position.

With two defeats against them questions were being asked both of Golden Miller and Gerald Wilson's ability to master and control him, just as questions had been asked of Billy Stott's ability. Golden Miller was regarded with such esteem, especially by his owner and trainer, that if he failed to win a race the blame must be put on the jockey not the horse, and not as would ultimately be deemed more worthy on owner and trainer, for over-racing the poor animal. Those questions of Wilson's ability were answered on 7 March and thoroughly ridiculed by the end of the season.

Cheltenham on Gold Cup Day saw slippery going, rain having fallen on hard ground. It was a talented field of seven runners: Kellsboro Jack, Inverse, Royal Ransom, Avenger, Delaneige, and the French horse El Haljar being the others, but none could master Golden Miller at his favourite course. Winning by an easy six lengths Golden Miller had beaten the record set by Easter Hero in 1930 of two successive victories by winning his third title. The praise rained down on both jockey and horse and it was written that 'Wilson's style exactly suits such a horse, since the great determination of one precisely balances the natural eagerness of the other in a fight'.

Sixteen days later Golden Miller and Gerald Wilson were lining up for the Aintree Grand National. With good going, Really True started as the 7/1 favourite with Golden Miller second favourite at 8/1. Wilson guided the Miller through the early part of the race with great mastery, not pushing too soon and allowing him to settle at a steady pace. Gregalach made the early running, but Wilson kept his horse well back. A mistake at Becher's almost ended the race for the Gold Cup winners, but Wilson held on and the Miller managed to recover himself after running along the ground on his knees with his nose almost touching the ground for a few yards. Then at the start of the second circuit, Wilson and Golden Miller surged to the front landing over the seventeenth a little ahead of Gregalach and Delaneige. At Valentine's the Miller and Delaneige were jumping with Forbra and Thomond II. Delaneige then took a slight lead and held it until the last when he jumped and landed with the Miller, but then lost the race as Wilson allowed the mighty horse to sprint away to the finish five lengths ahead, Thomond II finishing behind Delaneige. For the first and so far only time in history the two greatest races in British National Hunt were won by the same horse in the same season; furthermore the horse had broken the race record by eight seconds in the process, a record that had only been set the previous year when Kellsboro Jack won the race, but would then stand until Red Rum and Crisp's epic encounter of 1973.

That night Dorothy Paget held a fabulous party at the Adelphi hotel in Liverpool, which Gerald Wilson had to leave before its early morning finish as he had riding engagements the next day – he finished second in the Champion Steeplechase on a horse called Kakuskin. After finishing the day's racing he then

Gerry Wilson being led out for the Cheltenham Gold Cup on Golden Miller, 1935.

Gerry Wilson posing on Golden Miller after their Grand National win together, 1934.

caught a train home. Disembarking at Rugby he was mobbed by the public and carried shoulder-high out of the station by the lads from Fenny Compton.

The following year Gerry Wilson rode in that epic race at Cheltenham against Billy Speck on Thomond II which is now part of racing folklore, but the Grand National that followed it brought him to a period of his racing career that caused him great anguish. The Gold Cup on hard ground and at such a pace clearly took it out of Golden Miller, yet for most of the first circuit of the National he was looking the part of a heavily backed favourite. He was not jumping as well as he could and he was perhaps taking a little longer to get into his stride, but he was lying in a good third position at the rails when coming to the last ditch on the first circuit, the second fence after Valentine's. Here he suddenly pulled himself up as if he had lost confidence in himself, his head fell forward towards the bottom of the ditch and Gerry Wilson was thrown up the horse's neck, and then quite extraordinarily Golden Miller seemed to change his mind and jumped the obstacle from a standing position, but screwing to the left, totally unbalancing Wilson and throwing him out of his saddle.

Immediately the critics were out in force, forgetting all the masterful races Wilson had ridden. Faults were found in his technique and disgraceful insinuations were made that could have broken a lesser man. That evening Wilson was asked whether Golden Miller should be raced the next day in the Champion Steeplechase. He stated that he didn't want the horse to run as he felt he had been overworked on the hard ground and was not right. Basil Briscoe dismissed any suggestion of the Miller not being right and Dorothy Paget, with complete disregard for the horse's health, wanted him to race and bring her another prize. Furthermore Briscoe came to believe that Wilson had perhaps taken a bribe to throw the Grand National and told Dorothy Paget that he didn't want him to ride Golden Miller in the race. Dorothy Paget told Briscoe that she was the owner, that Wilson was her choice and that he would ride.

Golden Miller ran through the first fence of the Champion Chase instead of jumping it and Gerry Wilson went straight over his head on to his injured left shoulder.

For a short while Gerry Wilson continued to ride without being able to raise his arm above shoulder level while during the same period suffering sometimes terrible heckling from race crowds convinced that he had deliberately fallen from the Miller. Things came to a head in a race at Ludlow when he was on the favourite Abbott's Glance. Frenchie Nicholson who was also in the race took the wrong course and took Wilson with him. The reception was horrendous, with booing even emanating from the Members' Enclosure.

For a while afterwards Wilson gave up racing to sort his shoulder out. It was X-rayed again and under anaesthetic finally put right. Then on 31 August 1935, having recuperated and regained much of the strength in his arm, he married Vera Rimell, the daughter of Kinnersley trainer Tom Rimell who had saddled Forbra to win the 1932 National, and sister of Fred Rimell, the soon-to-be champion jockey and later master trainer, at Severn Stoke in Worcestershire. Fellow jockey Danny Morgan was his best man. They started their honeymoon at Teignmouth from where Gerry Wilson was perfectly situated to ride in the West Country meetings, winning three races at Totnes the Wednesday after his wedding, and then finished their honeymoon at Perth where he rode more winners.

He took a retainer for the next season with owner Mr G. Whitelaw whose trainer was Arthur Stubbs at Wantage, with the understanding that if Dorothy Paget wanted him to ride Golden Miller he would be allowed to do so.

After the Liverpool disaster, Basil Briscoe told Dorothy Paget that he would no longer train her horses and that if she didn't have them collected post-haste he would turn them loose. Her horses then went to Owen Anthony, and Basil Briscoe became and died a broken, impoverished man. To her credit the Hon. Miss Paget didn't subscribe to the view of Wilson ever taking a bribe, even before newsreel footage had completely exonerated him of any blame in his National fall, and so he was asked to ride Golden Miller at Newbury in the Andover Handicap Steeplechase the following season. They won convincingly in heavy going from Borris Band and Delapaix. Their next race together was to be their last; it was the Newbury Steeplechase in which there was a deliberate plan to stop the horse. The Miller was carrying a massive 12 stone 9 lb, and although he jumped well he couldn't get in front of a wall of horses that was blocking his route. Trailing further back from the leaders he was eventually forced to jump over the wing of a fence because it was so crowded. Wilson broke a finger but Golden Miller was unscathed. Hillsbrook ridden by W.T. O'Grady won the race. Dorothy Paget then decided that a new jockey was required and when Golden Miller won the Gold Cup for the fifth time it was with Evan Williams in the saddle. Wilson's mount Fouquet fell at the first ditch.

For six successive years Gerald Wilson was champion jockey, an achievement made in no small part by the fact that he was prepared to travel great distances to ride. One time he rode four races at Cartmel (of which two were winners) on Whit Monday and then travelled to Cardiff to ride one loser the next day. Frequently he would drive over 100 miles paying his own expenses, only to have a nasty fall or just be beaten, with the trainer and owner being dissatisfied and grumbling, and ending up out of pocket for his day's work.

He was only prevented from making it seven championships in a row on the last day of the 1938/9 season. The die was cast on 30 May with the race meeting at Newport. Both Gerry Wilson and his brother-in-law Fred Rimell were level in the jockeys' championship with 58 winners, and both had rides in the day to win the championship outright. Fred Rimell was booked to ride Caduminosa in the Blaina Handicap Steeplechase, but with no other competitors was awarded a walk-over. Wilson had a mount, Magic Island, in the Priory Novices' Hurdle

Roman Hackle in Charlton Drive, Cheltenham, the home of Gerry Wilson and his family shortly before and during the war.

Gerry Wilson on the left talking to his brother-in-law and first jockey Fred Rimell during a day's racing, c. 1946.

Owdeswell Manor at Andoversford, Gerald Wilson's training establishment that brought on such horses as Brains Trust, Last of the Dandies, Armoured Knight and Radiance.

Race but it failed to impress and finished fifth. In the third race, the Pontypool Steeplechase, both jockeys had rides, Wilson on Papageno and Rimell on Custom House: Rimell won with Wilson third. Rimell now had 60 winners to Wilson's 58 and of the three remaining races both jockeys only had mounts in the fourth race, the Tredegar Juvenile Handicap Hurdle Race. Rimell couldn't be beaten but still won this race on China Fox, Wilson being unplaced. Wilson had lost the championship in one final day's racing, but in effect the season had been lost earlier when he had been forced out of action for five weeks after a nasty fall when his horse fell on top of him, breaking five ribs and puncturing a lung with two of them.

Shortly after getting married Gerald and his wife Vera moved from his home at Wing to Cheltenham to a house in Charlton Drive that he named Roman Hackle, after the original and less successful horse by that name. Then, on 22 August 1936, almost a year after their wedding, the Wilsons celebrated the birth of their first and only child, a daughter they named Jane.

In 1939, five years after he had guided Lion Courage past Billy Parvin on Advancer to win the Imperial Cup he won his second Imperial Cup, this time on Prince Aly Khan's Mange Tout which was trained by perhaps the greatest hurdle jockey of all time, George Duller.

When the war broke out, Gerald Wilson was affected as deeply as most other jump jockeys, although he did manage to regain the champion jockey title after two years of relinquishing it to Fred Rimell. In the 1940/41 season with racing blighted by the war it was with a tally of just 22 winners that he won his last title.

He was rejected from joining the armed services because of all the racing injuries that he had endured, but he became an active member of the Home Guard and for a time worked on an assembly line at the Gloster Aircraft Company at Brockworth, a job that he detested and which he was delighted to give up to work on a farm.

When the war was coming to a close, he invested his money in Owdeswell Manor and its hundred or so acres of farmland just eastwards of Cheltenham at Andoversford, where he planned to go into training.

His first training season was an incredible success. National Hunt racing returned after its wartime break on 6 January 1945 at Cheltenham. At that first meeting he didn't have any winners, but then at Windsor on 10 February he won the first and last races of a nine-race programme with Brains Trust and Radiance respectively, both horses being ridden by Fred Rimell. He then went on to have a total of eleven winners in that season in which only nine days of racing were held, the horses doing the main honours being Brains Trust, Radiance, Albion and Sir Walter. Six of these winners all came during three days of racing in March at Cheltenham, the most significant of which was the Champion Hurdle on 31 March which Fred Rimell won on Brains Trust. This made him the first person to ride and train winners of the Champion Hurdle.

The trainer and his staff at Owdeswell Manor. Standing, from left to right: Clippy Stevens, Malcolm Smith, Derek Winters, Fred Isaacs (blacksmith), Taffy, Bill Denson, Sid Barnes, John Mastin, Spike Birch, Gordon Hart. Seated: Joe Malone, Mrs Wilson, Jane Wilson and Gerald Wilson.

The following season Carnival Boy came to his stables to continue Wilson's impressive start as a trainer. The horse won a flat race at Worcester on 19 October 1945 and then went on to win five hurdle races, the first of which was the Cowley Novices' Hurdle Race at Cheltenham on 10 November and the fifth at Windsor on 8 December. Then, with Fred Rimell, Wilson's first jockey, in the saddle he went on to finish second to Distel in the Champion Hurdle.

For almost a dozen years, backed by owners such as George Dowty, the Earl of Rosebery, Major D.J. Vaughan and Capt. D.L. Colville, Gerald Wilson kept a yard of up to forty horses (on occasion the stables at the Andoversford Hotel had to be utilised when Owdeswell Manor was overstocked!) that boasted such talent as Armoured Knight who won seven races for George Dowty between October 1948 and March 1951, Rightun, Browned

Gerald Wilson, trainer.

Off, Brush Off, Tintern Abbey and First of the Dandies. The last of these almost gave Wilson a Grand National winner in just his third year of training. In the 1948 Grand National First of the Dandies was partnered by Jimmy Brogan who thought he had won the race after jumping the last, and stopped riding him. Arthur Thompson on Sheila's Cottage saw the opportunity to get up on the rails and stole the race by a head.

The first apprentice taken on by Gerry Wilson was Malcolm Smith, who joined the stables in April 1945. Three months later he was given his first ride in a flat race at Salisbury where he jockeyed Brains Trust, of all horses. Earning just 2s 6d per week life as an apprentice at Owdeswell Manor was not overpaid, and Wilson was a hard taskmaster who demanded from his lads and apprentices the same work ethic that he had grown up with and had adhered to all his life. Nevertheless, Wilson was a fair man and gave all his apprentices and lads a good background from which they could further their careers. Malcolm Smith went on to have a racing career that lasted over twenty years, riding winners both on the flat and over jumps. Wilson's travelling head lad was Bill Denson, a jockey who could claim a number of winners and who would himself later go on to train in the Cheltenham area.

Gerald Wilson as landlord of The Marquis of Granby.

The stables were always a hive of activity; occasionally Pat Smythe came to ride out and help break in horses for the Gloucestershire Dairy, and most of the top jockeys would come and help school the horses that they hoped to ride.

In 1956 Wilson sold Owdeswell Manor, and retired from training. Ultimately, despite his success and the number of horses that he was given to train, he had found it too difficult to cover all his expenses and make a good, sustainable income from training and farming. He did have hopes of training privately for a Mrs Parsons of Newmarket but he was refused a private trainer's licence by the Jockey Club, so instead he bought a pub at Newbury called The Marquis of

Three of Gerry Wilson's horses being taken out on to Clock Square, Andoversford; left to right: Malcolm Smith on Dark Wonder, Pat Morrissey, and Donald Britten on Lady Chadwick.

Granby and became a landlord. A pub was an unusual acquisition for a man who was quite an introvert and certainly didn't crave attention, but he enjoyed life as a publican, and largely because of his hard work and ability as a raconteur, he proved most successful.

In the winter of 1968 Gerald Wilson became quite ill and at Christmas time his health deteriorated. He died, still at the Marquis, on 29 December 1968. The letters of condolence flooded to his widow from all over the country and all over the world, and from all levels of society. Later, his ashes were scattered along Cheltenham's racecourse, the venue of so many of his memorable wins. His wife Vera survived him until 1 May 1995.

5

Tim Hamey

Born in Grantham, Essex, on 17 December 1905, James Henry Hamey moved to Bishops Cleeve at the age of eighteen, having been an apprentice jockey to three different trainers by the age of sixteen, the last of whom was Lt-Col. Verschoyle. At this same age he had to give up riding on the flat when making the weight became too much of a problem. Although a short career, his flat-racing life brought him two victories, the first one being at Leicester on 12 April 1922 in the Gopsall Selling Stakes when his mount Pandarus beat Special jockeyed by J. Swaine, with the great Steve Donoghue on Pommel in third place. His second victory was just five days later on 17 April at Birmingham in the Bromsgrove Selling Plate on a horse called Cushy. Tobermory was second with Charlie Smirke.

He rode his first race over jumps at Birmingham on Monday 27 November 1922 on a horse called Castlerobin in the Coleshill Steeplechase over three miles. Of the eight runners they finished sixth. When the trainer he was retained to began cutting back on his jumpers Hamey moved to Bishops Cleeve where he took up lodgings at The Royal Oak pub, joining Captain Kirk's stable at Cleeve Hill. After a while he moved on to Newmarket before returning to Bishops Cleeve and Gloucestershire to ride for Arthur Saxby who was training in the village.

During his riding career he rode for many different trainers, intermittently even riding as a freelance jockey – a job that remains hard to this day, but during that interwar period was incredibly tough. Many trainers and owners wouldn't book riders until the race meeting and there were none of the agents there are today booking rides for you. Often Hamey would turn up at a meeting without a booked ride but would end up riding three or four mounts. Before the Second World War jockey fees were quite poor, particularly when it is considered that a jockey could be out of action for a lengthy spell if he had a bad fall. If the winner of a race received less than 85 sovereigns, then the losing jockeys would get three guineas and the winning jockey five. At this time perhaps four races on a card would be advertised as being worth 100 sovereigns; however, ten of these would go to the second place, five to third and with perhaps two going to the entry fee it would mean that the winner would only get about 83 sovereigns! Following the war this system was changed so that jockeys got seven guineas a ride irrespective of the value of the race.

As his face became more familiar on the race circuit John Henry Hamey adopted the name 'Tim' by which he would be known for the rest of his life. His first winner in National Hunt racing would come at the Market Rasen Union

Hunt meeting the April after his first ride over jumps. Monday 2 April 1923 was the date and the race that he won was the Town Hurdle Race over two miles. His horse was named Righlina and they won by just three-quarters of a length from R. Lyall on Have a Care. In the previous race Tim Hamey had come tantalisingly close to recording his first winner slightly earlier, by finishing second on Fardree in the two mile Selling Hurdle Race. A month later on 3 May Hamey recorded another victory on Mr H. Stokes' Righlina by winning the Hexham Handicap Hurdle Race. By the end of that year he had recorded five winners from 39 mounts. The following year was less successful – he had just three winners out of 36 rides – but in 1925 he was booked for twice the number of rides and scored 11 winners, not an earth shattering breakthrough, but nevertheless a significant enough tally to ensure that he was kept in touch with owners and trainers. Later, he was offered the post of second jockey for Jack Anthony, a position that he was pleased to take up and one which allowed him a little more comfort in knowing that he was certain of a number of rides each year.

The National Hunt season of 1925/26 was the first that was categorised as such, running over the autumn and winter of 1925 to the winter and spring of 1926, just as it is today. Previously each racing year for National Hunt was recorded January to December. The season would be a memorable one for Hamey, not least because it would be the one in which he was offered his first and only ride in the Cheltenham Gold Cup.

First run in 1924, the Cheltenham Gold Cup was still in its infancy and the prize money on offer to the winning owners was only £880 in 1926. Nevertheless the race aspired to the greatness that it would later be rewarded with and Tim was grateful for the mount that he believed was a great racehorse. Koko was owned by Frank Barbour from Trimblestown in County Meath, who also had in his stable Easter Hero, and was trained by A. Bickley. He was unfancied in the Gold Cup, going out at 10/1 in a field of just eight, largely because of the horse's erratic jumping, but he possessed speed and liked to race from the front, two qualities that Hamey was very aware of. Subsequently Tim Hamey rode the race that the horse wanted. From the outset he gave Koko his head and allowed him to make the front running. As a consequence the horse never looked like being beaten, he jumped with accuracy and speed; the other horses were never allowed to get near enough to unbalance or trouble him. This intelligent riding on Hamey's behalf brought Koko first past the post by an easy four lengths from Old Tay Bridge ridden by J. Hogan, with Ruddyglow, the heavily backed favourite partnered by his owner W. Filmer Sankey, a further three lengths behind.

The following day, 10 March, Tim Hamey won the Cheltenham Grand Annual Steeplechase on Black Miner from Jargoon with Dick Rees and Clashing Arms ridden by Jack Anthony. Again the race was a spectacle of Tim Hamey's horsemanship. Clashing Arms had done all the running when four fences from home Dare All in the following pack fell. This gave Hamey the chance to push Black Miner up the outside. Between the last two fences he wrested the lead from Clashing Arms and went on to win by four lengths. Once again in the space of two days he had taken an unfancied horse (Black Miner started at odds of 9/1) to beat a very strong favourite into third place.

Tim Hamey on Black Miner winning the 1926 Cheltenham Grand Annual Steeplechase from Jargoon with Dick Rees and Clashing Arms with Jack Anthony.

These Cheltenham Festival victories were invaluable to the young jockey. It brought him the recognition that was needed in the business and rides began to come much more freely. From this point Tim Hamey became one of the busiest jockeys on the circuit and gradually achieved a standard of living indicative of success. He would pick up 136 mounts for that season, and the following season would have 236. As well as the number of winners it is also the number of mounts that indicate a jockey's standing at the time. Those that are deemed talented will always pick up more rides, if not necessarily more winners, for optimistic owners and trainers will often book respected jockeys to ride their no-hopers in the hope that the jockey can make them perform above their abilities. Such was Hamey's increasing esteem. It is interesting to note that in the 1926/7 season Hamey secured more rides than either of his great friends Billy Stott and Billy Speck, if not more winners.

In July 1926 Tim Hamey married a young local girl named Phyllis Pullen, the daughter of Arthur and Sarah Pullen, who lived at Yew Tree Farm in the small village of Gotherington about a mile from Bishops Cleeve. Sarah's sister Olive was also destined to marry a jockey; she married the locally based Len Lefebve. Tim and Sarah were married at the Winchcombe register office and later set up home together in the bungalow on the Cheltenham Road in Bishops Cleeve that

The Gloucester Cavalcade of Sport with King Charles and his famous jockeys, 1930s. Jockeys in costume from left to right: Len Lefebve, Gerry Wilson, Tim Hamey and Fred Rimell.

Tim Hamey had had built, and which he had named Ardeen after a favourite mount. The neighbour of the Hameys was his friend Billy Stott, with another, Billy Speck, living a short distance away in the same village.

A few weeks after winning the 1926 Gold Cup, Tim Hamey was given the ride again on Koko, this time in the Aintree Grand National, a race that he would go on to feature in for twelve successive years. The first day of the Liverpool Meeting augured well for the Grand National, as Hamey finished second on Lotus Land in the Stanley Chase with the handicap of a broken stirrup iron.

However it was an inauspicious start to his sequence of Grand National rides the next day as Koko fell at Becher's Brook on the first circuit. The following year his horse Lissett III would also fall in the race, and his mount of 1928 (the year when only two of the forty-two runners finished) – Ardeen – failed to finish the race. Then in 1929, Hamey was given the ride on Grakle, a horse so spirited that he once took his jockey, Eric Foster, off the Ludlow course and towards the town, and for which a cross noseband was designed to control him! Today it is named after him. Despite his strength of character and wayward tendencies, Grakle was a horse of undisputed talent; he would go on to race in four Gold Cups, finishing second twice and third once and would feature in six consecutive Grand Nationals. In 1929 it was the third time that Grakle and the fourth that

Grand National and Cheltenham Gold Cup winning jockey John Henry (Tim) Hamey.

Hamey had raced in the National. Neither had achieved anything in the race to that point; Hamey largely out of bad luck, Grakle because the jockeys hadn't been able to control him enough to survive the course. There were 66 runners in the race that year and through his considerable horsemanship Tim Hamey brought Grakle home in one piece in sixth place, Gregalach taking the honours from Easter Hero. In 1930 Grakle was ridden by Keith Piggott in the National while Hamey had Harewood, who like Ardeen didn't finish the course, then in 1931 Tim Hamey was again meant to have the ride on Grakle.

Misfortune struck in the National Trial at Newbury when Grakle's erratic jumping resulted in Hamey having to go to hospital for some stitches in his head. Grakle's owner, Cecil Taylor, didn't think that Hamey would be fit enough for the National ride and duly booked Bob Lyall in his place. As it transpired Tim Hamey was fit enough and hugely disappointed to have been taken off the horse, but was still able to pick up another ride in the race – Solanum, who was yet another of Hamey's fallers. This was fated to be Grakle's year and the horse won it without Hamey, one-and-a-half lengths from Gregalach. Cecil Taylor however remembered the hard work that Hamey had done on the horse and his original commitment for him to ride Grakle and generously sent him a photograph of the horse along with a £50 consolation present.

If 1931 was Grakle's National, then 1932 was Hamey's. For his seventh attempt in the race he was offered the ride on Forbra, a horse on which he had finished third in the National Hunt Steeplechase at Cheltenham at the beginning of March and which was owned by bookmaker and Ludlow town councillor, William Parsonage. Forbra was trained by Tom Rimell at the Kinnersley stables in Worcestershire that would one day bring such great training success to his son Fred and daughter-in-law Mercy Rimell.

Originally Forbra was aimed at the Stanley Steeplechase on the first day of the National Meeting, but he was ruled out of this when he won a race at Taunton. Fortunately Tom Rimell had also entered him for the Grand National, and so it was decided to give the horse a chance for glory.

The last fence of the 1932 Grand National with Tim Hamey leading the way on Forbra.

Nearest the camera, Tim Hamey riding Negro, the dual Imperial Cup winner.

Forbra started the race completely unfancied at 50/1 in a field of 36, the smallest field in the National since 1926. From the start Hamey rode a waiting race from the front concentrating on getting Forbra to jump as well as he could. Evolution was the first leader but he fell at the Canal Turn; Egremont then took up the lead with his amateur rider Edward Paget. As the race progressed and the number of fallers increased the race became a two horse duel between Forbra and Egremont. After the last fence Hamey let Forbra go and the horse was never going to be beaten – he won by three lengths from Egremont with Shaun Goilin a bad third, and only eight finished in total. The 1932 Liverpool meeting was quite a successful one for Tim Hamey; as well as the Grand National win he had a third placing on Sansolena in the Lancashire Hurdle, a third on Tin o' Mint in the Liverpool Hurdle and a second in the Champion Chase on Brave Cry.

Forbra gave him a sixth placing in the Grand National in 1933 but he had nothing to celebrate for his remaining four runs, Lone Eagle II pulled up in 1934, Royal Ransom in 1935, Brienz in 1936 and his last, Delaneige in 1937 all fell. Nevertheless a first and two sixths in twelve successive runs is not a bad statistic for a race and a course that was then (and still is today, to a lesser degree) so punishing and merciless.

In his fifteen years of riding he notched up a total of 336 winners over fences and two on the flat. He was a consistent jockey who regularly rode over twenty winners a season – a seemingly low total, but significant when the champions of those seasons were only winning around about 80 of their races. Statistically over

The day after Tim Hamey's Grand National victory on Forbra he posed with friends at his home Ardeen on the Cheltenham Road in Bishops Cleeve. Tim is in the middle and is flanked by the 'two Billys', Speck on the left and Stott on the right.

his whole career he rode an average of one winner for every nine rides. His best two seasons were 1931/2 when he rode forty-one winners and 1934/5 when he rode forty. Apart from his association with Koko and Forbra he was also partnered several times with Gib and Negro, the latter of which won the February Hurdle at Newbury in 1933, ran third in the Lancashire Hurdle of the same year and won the Anglesey Hurdle Race in February 1935.

When Tim Hamey retired from riding it was with the intention of moving into training – an occupation that he hoped would have more financial security than riding, an important consideration now that he had a wife and would soon have two young boys to support. Although never very seriously injured in his riding career (he did break a collar-bone in the Scottish Grand National), the risk was always there that his income would be instantly curtailed by a bad fall. Unfortunately for small trainers there are still financial risks involved, albeit of a different nature, and ones which Hamey would get to know all too well.

He started training in 1938 in Bishops Cleeve, and among his early stable stars was Free Choice owned by S.T. Freeman. Free Choice gave Hamey his first winner at Cheltenham as a trainer, when with Frenchie Nicholson in the saddle he won the Winchcombe Selling Handicap Steeplechase on 28 December 1938. He briefly moved to Ombersley in Worcestershire and then in May 1939 he was offered the use of some stables named The Towers at Aston Clinton, and for a short period moved his operation there until the war changed his plans.

In 1942 Tim Hamey was called up for war service and became number 10693301, Sergeant James Henry Hamey of the 433 Company Horse Transport, Royal Army Service Corps. He took initial training at Boscombe Down and was then sent to the Middle East. He would serve his country for three and a half years, a period in which his wife, Phyllis, would first of all take work at the newly opened Smith's factory in Bishops Cleeve as an inspector and then go on to work for the Ministry of Labour.

When Tim returned home in 1946 he and his family had to start again from scratch. During the war his wife and two sons John and Rex had been living back with her parents at Yew Tree Farm in Gotherington. He moved them temporarily into the officers' mess of the Stoke Orchard aerodrome and then, starting with just four horses, he moved into Moat Farm, Park Lane, in Prestbury. This was an ideal place to train from, especially for a small trainer such as Hamey. It quite literally backed on to the Cheltenham Racecourse, and Prestbury at that time was a centre for horseracing, with trainers and jockeys in abundance. A short distance away was Cleeve Hill upon which Tim Hamey and the other local trainers could carry out the daily exercising of their charges. Prestbury was a small village with a strong sense of community; there was no animosity for many years towards the regular appearances of racehorses on the small roads.

For twelve years Tim Hamey trained from Prestbury. The number of horses averaged about fourteen and, for an enterprise that was so small and relied so heavily on a small number of patrons, he was constantly in fear of his bills not being paid. There were occasions when owners might suffer losses in the city or indeed on the racetrack, and when clearing their debts it was often the case that the smaller trainer such as Hamey would be left with his bill unpaid or paid late. This cashflow problem was and is still today a constant worry for small trainers.

Nevertheless Tim Hamey managed to continue his business and occasionally was able to put out winners such as Chainlink, who won 17 from 36 starts in a career that was partly under the care of Hamey. In the 1952/3 season they won five races together, three of which had Tim's son Rex Hamey on board. Another was Sahara, a horse that won two races in three days ridden by Rex. A third notable name in the Hamey stables was Baldachino, a horse owned by Jack and Percy King that Tim Hamey trained under permit to win the Severn Selling Hurdle Race at Cheltenham in October 1960, ridden by Terry Biddlecombe.

In 1958 after twelve years' training at Moat Farm, Tim Hamey was approached by Bryan Robinson from Pratt and Co. who at that time managed Cheltenham Racecourse, to tell him that they wanted to expand the course and in order to do so needed the land that Moat Farm was built on. It was a polite request but in reality it was a compulsory purchase by Pratt and Co., and Hamey had little say in the matter. With great regret he began to look for new premises to carry on training. Pratt and Co. gave him as much time as he needed until finally he decided to move to a bungalow in Brookthorpe-with-Whaddon, a small village a little south of Gloucester, from where Percy King offered him the opportunity to work as his private trainer.

Tim Hamey in retirement at Cheltenham Racecourse. He was for a time the oldest surviving Grand National winner and remained a regular race follower, becoming known as the 'Gentleman of Cheltenham'.

The Hameys then moved to Yew Tree Farm in Whaddon Green, kept a small number of horses in training and took to farming. By the mid-1970s with age taking its toll Tim eventually retired from training, but continued to work the farm. His wife Phyllis became ill and sadly died on 10 January 1988.

Tim carried on as best as he could, moving to Pullar Court in Bishops Cleeve where he could be cared for and looked after by his family better. He ever remained faithful to his love of racing and was a regular and welcome visitor to Cheltenham. Truly regarded in his latter years as the 'Gentleman of Cheltenham' he became the oldest surviving winner of the Gold Cup, a mantle that was taken over by Fulke Walwyn on 15 April 1990, Easter Sunday, when Tim passed away. He is buried in Bishops Cleeve churchyard.

6

Davy Jones

David Lewis Jones was born in Llanelli, Wales, on 17 April 1907, the fourth son of Thomas Jones, a haulier who lived in Copperworks Road. As a boy Davy Jones loved his father's horses and would take them down on summer nights to be turned out to graze in a nearby field. There was apparently a local butcher's pony that the young boy would occasionally get to ride, but the legend goes that it was at the tender age of ten that Davy Jones got his first paid ride, albeit not under rules. Seeing one of the local tradesmen's ponies turned out in a field pawing at the ground and snorting, the eldest of a group of young lads bet Davy a penny that he couldn't ride it. Without fear and always keen to make money – two qualities that remained with him throughout his life – the ten-year-old got on to the back of the pony, hoisted up by his comrades. With a slap on the animal's rump the boy was careering round the field. When the chase seemed to be ending the boys started to hurl lumps of soil at the horse to keep him going. Through it all the diminutive boy held on for his penny. Then a stone was inadvertently thrown and hit the jockey on the top of his head, his scalp split and blood gushed out of a wound whose scar would remain for the rest of the jockey's life. Recognising that the game had been played too long, the boys rushed up and grabbed the pony, calming it and stopping it. Davy tumbled off, blood all down his face and straining to stay conscious. He looked around him, stared the boy who had challenged him in the eye and said, 'Where's my bloody penny then?'

There was no family influence on the young Davy Jones to turn his hand to becoming a jockey. Indeed his family intended him to become a man of the cloth, following the path of his mother Ann's brother, who was Dean of Wrexham; or failing that follow the impressive steps of his mother's other brother who was the chairman of directors of Pearl Assurance.

Naturally intelligent, Davy passed the exams to enter Llanelli and Carmarthen County School, but he was anxious to leave and become a jockey. However, although even as a young teenager he was schooling local horses over fences, hurdles and banks, there didn't seem to be any opportunities open to him. Fate played its hand when after leaving school Davy found himself working alongside the brother of Ben Roberts, who was training in Cheltenham. He appreciated that Davy had a natural love of and prowess with horses and suggested that he write to his brother for a job. Jones did so and at the rather late age of eighteen joined the Ben Roberts stable in Windsor Street, Cheltenham, as an apprentice jockey in August 1925, taking up lodgings in Selkirk Terrace.

Davy Jones in his racing silks.

His first public ride came at Wolverhampton in early October 1925 on a horse named El Ray; then after just a couple of months with Roberts and in only his second race in public on 29 October he won the Coventry Apprentice Stakes at Worcester by a head, on a horse called Ridgeway. He would go on riding in races until he was sixty-five, extraordinarily having success throughout his career both on the flat and in National Hunt. He would experience racing all over the world, with races started at times in stalls, at the barrier gate, by elastic tape and by flag. He would race against Frenchie Nicholson, Fred Rimell, Gerry Wilson, Gordon Richards, Steve Donoghue, Lester Piggott, Joe Mercer and Paul Cook among many other stars from both sides of the racing world. Ultimately his career was not shrouded in glory, but his longevity as a jockey and the incredible changes that he saw and adapted to make him one of a unique band. He was always a very smart man and immaculately dressed, paying particularly great attention to the condition of his fingernails.

In winter 1927, two years after he had joined Ben Roberts, Davy Jones made his first trip abroad when he was invited to ride in Madras, India. The trek halfway across the world was an arduous one. Initially he had to take a boat over the Channel to Boulogne, then go on to Paris where he took a train down the length of the country to board a ship at Marseilles. This engaged on a two-week voyage to Bombay, and from Bombay he had another two days and a night's train journey to get to Madras. The Indian tracks still run by the British Raj brought some success and an association with the Sultan of Jahore for the tiny Welshman. He would recall that the Sultan had a palace stacked full of furniture made from glass, and tiger cubs roaming around like domestic cats.

After his Indian successes he succumbed to the rich food available on the two-week sea journey home and his weight ballooned up to 8 st 7 lb, too heavy to ride on the flat by the time he returned to England. Consequently he took out a licence to jump and rode his first races on Easter Monday in 1928. Even though

Davy Jones winning at Newton Abbot.

he had soon worked off the excess pounds he remained riding under both sets of racing rules until he was forty. Many of his National Hunt rides were at smaller meetings that have long since disappeared.

He rode with utter fearlessness and used a technique in his riding that brought him much success. He developed a wild scream that inevitably put his fellow jockeys off, and in the times before starting stalls he would often come charging from behind the field as the tapes went up, screaming terrifyingly. The result was often that the jockeys in front of him would part like the Red Sea to let him through. Throughout his career he was fairly lucky with being able to control his weight. Standing just 5 feet and 1 inch tall he had the solid, strong-shouldered build necessary to control the much bigger animals he was asked to ride, but weight would roll off him almost at will. If he had put on too much weight for a particular race he could burn off three or four pounds by running in a sweatsuit and sweaters. On one particular occasion he had to lose a couple of pounds in order to ride some lightweights at Newbury, so he put on the sweatsuit and turned the heaters up full blast in his car while driving to the course, and when he arrived he found that he had burned off six pounds and not just two!

He would continue to race abroad for the rest of his long career; as well as in Britain and India he rode in the Far East, Denmark, Kenya and the USA. It would become his habit to spend the summer in England and then go abroad for the winter, returning each year in time for the Cheltenham Festival. His first

*The last day of 1937 and racing at Newbury, with Davy Jones nearest the camera on
Adamant. The other horses from left to right are Vigilent, Kiang and Larigot.*

experiences of racing from stalls came in the States where he rode at Santa Anita
in California and in Florida at Hialeah and Gulfstream Park.

For several seasons Davy Jones was unable to really break into jump racing,
winning just one race in the 1932/3 season from nine races, nine the next season
from 62 mounts, thirteen in 1934/5 and sixteen in 1935/6. The next season he
broke into the twenties, achieving a tally of exactly 20 from 157 mounts; this set
him up for some impressive years over the jumps and the following year he got his
first ride in the Grand National.

In the Grand National of 1938 Davy Jones guided his mount, Red Knight II, a
horse he had ridden to win a four-mile race at Cheltenham and to finish as runner-
up to Fred Rimell on Teme Willow but in front of T. McNeill on Battleship in the
National Hunt Handicap Steeplechase at the Cheltenham Festival, over the
Aintree fences to come home in sixth place, behind the seventeen-year-old Bruce
Hobbs on Battleship. On Thursday 10 November 1938 he returned to Liverpool to
achieve the incredible feat of riding over hurdles, over fences and on the flat all on
the same day in a time when mixed meetings still took place there. The first race
was the Abbeystead Hurdle Race at 1 o'clock, which was won by Frenchie
Nicholson on Iceberg II; Jones came in eleventh on Speed Trap. Then at 2.10 the
Grand Sefton Chase went off with Jones on his Grand National mount, Red
Knight II, but unfortunately they fell and the race was won by T. Carey. The flat

race was the Wavertree Selling Handicap over one mile and five furlongs – Scotch Woodcock won with T. Weston, and Jones came in eighth on Le Kirghize.

A few months before this significant and historic achievement, on 12 June 1938, Davy was married at Burford to Kathleen Anne who has always been known simply as 'Nancy'. For his marital home he paid £850 cash for a house in Welland Lodge Road, Cheltenham, that had a brick-built garage and which he would name Ridgeway, after the horse that had brought him his first victory. He would keep this house for over fifty years, always returning to it after his winter excursions abroad.

The war years saw him engage in service for his country and so Davy Jones went to work on the production lines of the Gloster Aircraft Company at Brockworth, the same factory that Gerry Wilson was employed in.

David Lewis Jones and his new bride Kathleen at Burford, 12 June 1938.

Despite the wartime restrictions, however, Davy Jones did continue to race and the pinnacle of his racing career came towards the end of the Second World War on Saturday 17 March 1945, when he was engaged to ride Red Rower for Lord Stalbridge in the first Gold Cup run for three years, and the first and only Gold Cup that the jockey would ride in. Without a Grand National to look forward to that year and with National Hunt racing still in its infancy from its enforced wartime break, the Cheltenham Gold Cup was of huge interest and importance. Third in an eight-race programme, the Gold Cup attracted a record field of sixteen runners among which was Poet Prince, the 1941 winner, Rightun (now aged fifteen), who was placed third in 1940 and Red Rower, the runner-up in 1942 and third in 1941.

With only eleven racing days prior to the Gold Cup, form was hard to ascertain, but the punters made Red Rower the 11/4 favourite, with Paladin at 100/30 and Schubert at 11/2 second and third favourites respectively. Schubert made the initial running, being ridden by his trainer Chris Beechener. From the stands first time round to three fences from home Frenchie Nicholson on Poet Prince held the lead, then Schubert and Paladin, jumping in tandem, took over and to all intents and purposes it looked like a two-horse race. Then, suddenly at the last fence Davy Jones materialised on Red Rower, jumped past them and

The 1945 Champion Hurdle. Fred Rimell leads on the Gerry Wilson-trained Brains Trust who went on to win; just about to jump in second place is Davy Jones on Red April, who was beaten into third place by just three-quarters of a length by Don Butchers on Vidi.

raced up the hill to win by three lengths in a course record time of 6 minutes, 6.15 seconds – a misleading time as part of the course was turned over for wartime agricultural requirements and the race was a quarter of a mile shorter than usual. Being so heavily backed, the result was warmly welcomed by the crowd and Lord Stalbridge became the first to own and train the winner of the Gold Cup – a feat only duplicated once to date, in 1990 when S.G. Griffiths' Norton's Coin won at odds of 100/1. It was not however the first success for Lord Stalbridge, as he owned the 1927 winner of the Gold Cup, Thrown In, who was trained by Owen Anthony. He also owned and trained Bogskar who won the 1940 Grand National.

The perfectly timed attack by Davy Jones on Red Rower to win the Gold Cup and the overall tactics that he employed when the horse was not jumping at his best give him credit enough, but added to this must be considered the fact that as he was such a lightweight jockey, Davy Jones had to carry three stone of dead weight on the horse's back. Winning with this is surely a feat by both horse and man, but the remuneration that he received for such heroics was a mere £35; the prize money on offer that year was the lowest in its history before or since at just £340. In contrast, when Prince Regent won the Gold Cup the following year, the prize money was the highest it had ever been at £1,130.

Two weeks after the Gold Cup, Cheltenham hosted the Champion Hurdle in its last day of the season on Saturday 31 March. It was a day of racing that saw Fred Rimell win the first three races and four in total on the seven-race card. The third of those wins was on Brains Trust in the Champion Hurdle, which also saw Davy Jones record his best result in the race when riding again for Lord Stalbridge. He came in third out of sixteen runners on Red April, only one-and-a-half lengths behind the winner.

One week later Davy Jones was back to winning ways at Cheltenham by taking the Hatherley Handicap Steeplechase on Belisha from Fred Rimell on Jack Tar and G. Bowden on Alacrity. On 6 September 1945, less than six months after winning the Gold Cup, Jones weighed out at just 7 stone 10 lb to ride Sister Patricia in the Ebor Handicap at York. It was a closely contested race, Jones losing it by a neck to Harry Wragg on Wayside Inn.

Three years after his Festival successes the small Welshman retired from National Hunt racing to concentrate on the flat. At Haydock on 18 August 1948 he had the dubious distinction of finishing second in the £294 Wigan Lane Selling Handicap to a twelve-year-old Lester Piggott, weighing out at just 5 stone on The Chase in the first career win of a jockey who would win more Classics than any other and be second only to Gordon Richards in the table of Britain's most successful jockeys. Davy Jones and Lester Piggott would over the course of time have several tussles. Indeed, in that first win for Piggott the victor has since claimed that Davy Jones virtually gave him the race, helping to shout Piggott's mount home. On another occasion at Salisbury they were racing against each other again. Davy Jones was on a horse trained by Lester's father, Keith, a horse that Lester should have been riding but which he had turned down in favour of another that he fancied to win it. During the course of the race Davy got himself up on the inside of Piggott and pushed his elbow under the younger jockey's so that Lester couldn't use his whip properly. Jones then went on to win the race. Piggott was furious and complained bitterly to the stewards, but without the aid of the patrol cameras that there are now there was no evidence to back up the young jockey's claim, and Davy retained the race.

In 1949 Davy Jones had his most successful season, numerically speaking, riding 55 winners and finishing joint ninth in the jockeys' table. One of those wins was the Newbury Spring Cup on Coalition and four winners all came in one day on a card at Hamilton Park, a feat that he would duplicate nine years later at Chepstow when all four of his booked rides for the day came home first.

His other big flat winner in Britain was on Penitent in the 1954 Old Newton Cup, but in riding in three Derbys, 1946 on Hispaniola, 1948 on Black Pampas and 1951 on Faux Pas – all without success – he is only one of a select group of jockeys to have ridden in both the Grand National and the Derby. Ultimately it would be just the St Leger of the English Classics in which Davy Jones would not feature.

At Doncaster, the Welshman was involved in the Beechfield Handicap on Resistance and at the finishing post the judge couldn't separate his mount from that of William Nevett who was on Phantom Bridge, and a dead heat was declared. The historical relevance of this is that it was the first time on a British racecourse that a dead heat was announced when a photo-finish camera was in operation.

Jones rode his last race in Britain in 1966; indeed his last British winner came two weeks before his fifty-ninth birthday when he brought Bill Elsey's Tesica first past the post, but he continued to ride overseas until he reached the compulsory retirement age of sixty-five. In 1970 at the age of sixty-two Jones chalked up yet another memorable win in the Kenya Derby on Verre Doré, an

Davy Jones on Amphora being led to race in Nairobi. The horse was owned and trained by Mrs E. Harris.

Singapore, 21 February 1953: Davy Jones up on Box Office, a horse he had just ridden to success for Mrs Shaw who leads them in.

only slightly fancied horse that started the race at odds of 12/1. The following year he added to his tally that of the Guineas in the same country on a horse called Nimbus, beating Paul Cook's mount by half a length in the process. Eventually it was the racing stewards of Nairobi that effectively retired Davy Jones from racing, but he quickly found a new focus for his incredible energies and set up an academy for young Africans wanting to enter the racing world and emulate the small man from Llanelli. It was a short lived endeavour that did help some apprentices, but it was soon clear to the ageing horseman that his home lay back in the British Isles.

Refusing to retire completely he took up a position as assistant trainer to Jimmy Thompson for owner David Robinson. When that became too much he still managed to raise himself from his bed six mornings a week at 6.30 to be riding out by 7 for trainer Owen O'Neill – who still trains from Cleeve Lodge today. Cleeve Lodge is a small stables on Cleeve Hill previously used by Charlie Piggott and Bill Marshall, both of whom used Jones' services at some time or other. Later he rode out for Jim Perrett who trained a small string of horses from his yard in

Davy Jones winning the Alasirit Three Year Old Handicap in Kenya on Amphora from Higlass, Gooseberry, Hard to Beat and Rectangle, 26 September 1971.

Shipton Oliffe. Even after he had a hip replaced at the Royal Masonic Hospital Jones refused to down tools, and after a short period of convalescence he was once again riding out every morning. He was into his eighties before he eventually accepted full retirement.

On St David's Day, 1 March 1992 David Lewis Jones finally succumbed to the cancer that had attacked his spine and died aged 84 at the Pittville Lawn Nursing Home in Cheltenham that had been his last home. Ten days later on the middle day of the Cheltenham Festival his funeral was held at St Mary's Church in Prestbury. The organist played the theme to The Horse of the Year Show and mourners from throughout the racing world paid their last respects. On the Friday following, Davy's eldest son Peter took his father's ashes to the racecourse on which he had had his finest hour and sprinkled them on the course just in front of the stands at the approximate position of the old Gold Cup starting line.

Of his three sons, two followed their father into racing. Peter, who rode nearly two hundred winners in his career, was first associated with Bill Marshall when he worked out of Cleeve Lodge and later went on to have an excellent association

Davy Jones in his racing silks in France during the latter part of his racing career.

with Alec Kilpatrick, for whom he won races on Bassnet and won the Molyneux Chase at Liverpool on Leslie. The second son, Thomas Michael, known as Buck, held an apprenticeship with Sam Armstrong and in August 1959 won the 2 o'clock apprentice race at Salisbury on Hasty Hook. Half an hour later, in the next race at the same meeting, Buck's father won on a horse called Lemlem. Buck later took up National Hunt racing, winning the 1964 Imperial Cup on Invader, the 1966 Ansell's Brewery Handicap Chase on Shanlis and the 1971 Haydock Park Grand National Trial on The Otter. He took up a training licence in the 1969/70 season and today trains from his farm at Albury near Guildford.

7

Frenchie Nicholson

On Saturday 14 March 1942 in a National Hunt season so severely affected by wartime government restrictions and harsh weather that it would only hold eighteen days of racing, Cheltenham held the first day of its two-day National Hunt Festival. In order that there would be no interference with the working week, the second day was held the following Saturday. Each of the two days held one of National Hunt's great races: the 14th saw Ron Smyth bring Forestation first past the post in the Champion Hurdle and the 21st witnessed 'Frenchie' Nicholson powering Medoc II home by eight lengths from Red Rower to win the Cheltenham Gold Cup. The locally based jockey had won National Hunt's most prestigious prize.

Herbert Charles Denton Nicholson was born on 13 January 1913 in Maltby, near Rotherham, in Yorkshire. At that time Herbert's father, Harry Nicholson, was a farmer who also made some money from dealing in horses. In the years to come his employment would take him and his family from Yorkshire to the USA where he managed a stud farm in New Hampshire, to Cambridge where he ran a livery yard for undergraduates and to France where in Bordeaux he worked for an American, hunting his hounds. All this nation-hopping occurred in the first nine years of Herbert Nicholson's life, but by this age he was a mature enough rider to join with the leaders of the hunts.

Showing such ability in the saddle, his father decided that Herbert should be apprenticed as a flat race jockey to Charlie Clout in Lamorlaye in the South of France. So, at the age of just twelve, H.C.D. Nicholson went on his own to stay in a hostel in the French village to learn how to become a jockey. He was with Clout for a tenure of three years, during which time he picked up a few mounts, but his natural build was always going to be too much for him to become a successful jockey on the flat.

In 1928 he moved back to England where for seven years he was apprenticed at Treadwell House in Epsom, the residence of the trainer Stanley Wootton. It was here that Herbert Nicholson acquired the nickname that was to last him his lifetime and beyond, derived apparently from the fact that when he first turned up at Treadwell House he was wearing a French overcoat. Initially the other lads christened him 'Little Frenchie', but soon this became simply 'Frenchie'.

Stanley Wootton was the most respected man of his day in the field of jockey tutoring. He was a disciplinarian and a hard taskmaster (attributes that would one day be recognised in Frenchie) but he attained great results. His pupils read like a

Frenchie Nicholson, aged just seventeen, on The Torch at Hurst Park, 15 March 1930.

who's who of British horseracing in the first half of the twentieth century. Along with Frenchie, Harry Sprague (1956 Champion Hurdle winner), Vic Smyth (four-time winning trainer of the Champion Hurdle), Arthur Wragg and Staff Ingham among many others learned their trade with Wootton.

Wootton worked his apprentices hard – seven days a week with just one week's holiday a year. He paid them little, misdemeanours were not abided and his rules were not made to be broken. He insisted that his boys were polite, punctual and dressed properly. It was a hard life that Frenchie had come to but one which reaped its rewards. The tutoring that young jockeys received from Wootton was acknowledged in the racing world as being of a high calibre. 'Wootton' boys knew how to ride and so they were always in demand. They had been taught tactical riding, good riding posture and how to conserve a horse's strength for precisely the right moment.

Frenchie Nicholson soon began to realise his riding potential under Wootton's guidance and in 1929, at the age of sixteen, he rode in his first hurdle race. On 11 March 1930 he won his first race at Cheltenham, a course and a town that would have such importance in his future. The race was the Stayers Selling Hurdle Race in the Festival; it was on the same day that Tim Cullinan won the Champion Hurdle on Brown Tony and the Gold Cup on Easter Hero, in a year when both races were on the same Festival day. Cullinan also went on to win the Grand National on Shaun Goilin that year; this feat of winning all three races in the same season has not to date been equalled. Nicholson's ride was on his boss's own horse Sobrino and in winning the race he beat Billy Stott, the champion jockey, on Montpelier into second place. This was the first of 48 wins that Frenchie would go on to ride at Cheltenham, and just one of the ten that he would total in his first racing season. With just 27 rides that season it was a very respectable start to his career, and for the next four seasons he wouldn't be able to equal it, but then in 1934/5 his career took a turn for the better.

On 1 March 1935 he rode a treble at Gatwick with Porthaon in the Tantivy Chase, Victor Norman in the International Hurdle Race and Zanzibar in the Four Year Old Handicap Hurdle Race. Then he was offered his first Grand National mount, the Bertram Mills-owned Jimmy James. It would be his first of six appearances in the great steeplechase. He fell at the first fence in 1935 and never in any of the attempts did he complete the gruelling Aintree course: the best he achieved was falling at Becher's the second time. The year that Royal Mail won the National, 1937, saw Frenchie on Didoric. Momentarily they became stuck on the top of the Chair, and then as Didoric tried to continue the race Frenchie found himself hanging on to his mount from underneath the horse's neck.

Despite such an inauspicious record in the National, Nicholson was destined for other significant achievements in his chosen profession. By the end of the 1934/5 season he had ridden 39 winners from 216 mounts, more than the combined totals of his first five seasons, and he was beginning to carve out a name for himself as a solid dependable jockey.

The following season was plagued by injury. In accumulating a tally of 17 winners Frenchie spent three months on the sidelines with a broken leg. Then on Tuesday 10 March 1936 Nicholson rode his first race after breaking his leg. His mount in the Champion Hurdle was Victor Norman, a horse he had ridden the previous year in this same race, and he was only riding because of his

The Peascod Hurdle Race with Frenchie Nicholson and Fred Rimell, 8 December 1945.
Carnival Boy was trained by Gerry Wilson and finished second to Distel in the following year's
Champion Hurdle.

characteristic determination not to miss such an important race. The injury to his leg was in fact too serious for him to have come back to racing so soon, and as a consequence of the strain that he put on it prematurely he walked with a slight limp for the rest of his life. Nevertheless, Frenchie was set on riding Victor Norman, a grey who had finished fourth in the Champion Hurdle of the previous year, who was trained by the American, Morgan 'Bam' Blair and owned by Mrs Michael Stephens. Victor Norman was pedigree through and through: his sire was King Sol who had won the 1919 Stewards' Cup at Goodwood and his dam was Tickits who was herself sired by the mighty Trespasser, triple Imperial Cup winner from 1920 to 1922. He was bought by Michael Stephens in a seller on the flat at Alexandra Park for 230 guineas and then sent to Bam Blair to go over hurdles. Shortly before the Champion Hurdle Stephens died, and thus it was in the colours of his widow that Victor Norman ran.

The day's racecard opened with fog obliterating the racecourse, but through a combination of strong sunshine and a gusty wind the visibility was much improved by the time of the big race. Of the eight runners Free Fare ridden by Georges Pellerin was the horse that the punters were favouring and he started the race at odds of 5/2. Victor Norman was second favourite at 4/1. However, the race was all Victor Norman and Frenchie Nicholson. From the off they took the lead and jumped the hurdles with such speed and finesse that contemporary reports of the race ranked the horse alongside the great Trespasser. Three lengths in front of Free Fare at the finishing post, Victor Norman gave his jockey the most important win of his career thus far. For the 1937 Champion Hurdle Frenchie was once again asked to ride Victor Norman, the third time that they would ride together in the race. The race started like the previous year with Victor Norman taking the lead, but second from last he was finding it too much and the Dorothy Paget-owned horse Menton, the favourite Free Fare and Our Hope all took over the running. At the post it was Georges Pellerin on Free Fare who took the honours, Victor Norman and Nicholson trailing in fifth. That season of 1936/7 was an important one for Nicholson, however, as with just three wins fewer than Gerry Wilson's winning total of 45, he finished in third place in the jockeys' championship. It was also the year in which he met his bride to be, the beautiful Diana Holman, great-granddaughter of William Holman, the patriarch of the racing dynasty that played such a part in Cheltenham's racing history. In January 1938 they became engaged and then on 11 June of that year they were married at St Mary's Church in Prestbury. T.F. Carey was the best man and among the many guests were such racing names as Tim Hamey, Fred Rimell, Staff Ingham, Gerald Wilson and Fulke Walwyn. It was a well-publicised wedding, not because of the fame of the jockey, but for the high status held by the Holman family in the town. The Nicholsons set up their first home together at Woodcote Hurst, Epsom, but it wouldn't be too long before the Holman home town beckoned.

In the March before getting married Frenchie was given his first ride in the Cheltenham Gold Cup; the horse he was to partner was the legendary Golden Miller. The Paget-owned horse had already won the Gold Cup in five successive years between 1932 and 1936 as well as the 1934 Grand National; with the Gold

The wedding of Herbert Charles Denton Nicholson to Diana Holman at St Mary's Church, Prestbury, 11 June 1938.

Cup cancelled in 1937, the 1938 race would have brought the great horse a sixth successive title. Frenchie had first ridden Golden Miller at Birmingham in 1937 when they won by fifteen lengths, and he would surely have ridden him if the Gold Cup had taken place in that year. Then in early 1938 he won two more races on the Miller, the first at Sandown on 13 January when they won the Prince's Handicap Chase by three-quarters of a length from Gerry Wilson on Sporting Piper, and six weeks later on 28 February they won the Optional Selling Chase at Birmingham by twenty-five lengths from Irish Briar – they proved to be the horse's last wins and achievements that Nicholson was always very proud of.

On 10 March 1938, two days after Frenchie had ridden Lobau to third place in the Champion Hurdle and the day after he had won the National Hunt Juvenile Chase on Medoc II, Golden Miller lined up as 7/4 favourite with Morse Code, Macauley, Southern Hero, Airgead Sios and Red Hillman to contest the Gold Cup. The entire race was largely contested between Frenchie on the Miller and Danny Morgan on Morse Code. Even at the last fence there was little between them, then on the final race up the hill to the finishing post the Miller's age finally caught up with him and, gallant to the last, he was beaten for the first time in his career at Cheltenham. Morse Code took the honours two lengths ahead of Golden Miller with Macauley a further three lengths behind.

A fortnight later on 24 March Nicholson won the Coronation Hurdle race on Santayana at Liverpool. That season was his most impressive to date. He finished second in the jockeys' table with Gerry Wilson taking his sixth successive title. Wilson finished with 59 winners, Nicholson with 54, but incredibly in amassing his total Frenchie rode 110 fewer mounts than Wilson, resulting in a win rate for Nicholson of less than one in five, with Wilson's rate at over one in six.

On 19 March 1939 the Nicholsons celebrated the birth of their first child, a boy whom they named David. Four days later David's father won the Coronation Hurdle at Liverpool on Master Matty, and then fell from Montrejeau II in what would prove to be his penultimate Grand National.

Shortly after the war broke out on 3 September 1939 they decided that Epsom was not the safest place to raise a family, and so they moved to Lake House in Prestbury to stay with Diana's parents. Diana had been brought up in Prestbury and Lake House had been in her family since her grandfather Frederick acquired it at the turn of the century. By Diana returning to Cheltenham the continuance of a great local racing dynasty which started over a century before was assured. Her husband Frenchie would take over the mantle of racing success and in time her son David would carry it further.

The outbreak of war saw great confusion in the sporting world as a whole. The initial reaction of all in government was to stop all sporting activities, and even recreational activities such as dances were stopped and theatres and cinemas were closed. However, as the Phoney War progressed it was soon realised that it was necessary to keep the morale of the public high and so cinemas and theatres were reopened and sports allowed to continue. Nevertheless the racing calendar remained deeply affected with very many meetings being cancelled. The War Department took over such courses as Aintree and the Grand National was not run between 1941 and 1945. Cheltenham racecourse was taken over first by

H.C.D. Nicholson and Golden Miller on their way out for the 1938 Gold Cup.

Frenchie Nicholson up on Henri's Choice, winning the Champion Steeplechase at the Cheltenham Festival.

British servicemen and then American soldiers, but continued to hold sporadic race meetings up to March 1942 when it staged its last Festival until 1945. For jockeys and trainers making a living under these circumstances was nigh on impossible. Many of course did not have to as they were enlisted to fight and serve their country. Frenchie desperately wanted to join up but was refused on medical grounds – the fractures that he had incurred in his career made him unfit for active service. Instead he signed up for the Prestbury Home Guard, which met at the Women's Institute Hall, turned his hand to a bit of farming, which he happened to have a gift for, and continued to ply his trade as a professional jockey.

He was third for a second time in the Champion Hurdle in 1941, this time on Ephorus. In March 1942 Frenchie was offered his second ride in the Gold Cup, this time on Lord Sefton's Medoc II. As the Festival was being run over two separate weekends, many of the horses entered for the Gold Cup that was to take place on the second Saturday were also entered in the Cheltenham Grand Annual Steeplechase to be held on the first Saturday. That race became seen as a dress rehearsal for the real event. Danny Morgan on Red Rower won the race from Frenchie on Medoc II and Broken Promise in third. Immediately Red Rower was seen as the favourite for the Gold Cup.

Frenchie Nicholson on Ursulus just stretching slightly ahead of Fred Rimell on Carnival Boy in the Peascod Hurdle Race at Windsor. Although Ursulus took a slight lead two hurdles out, Carnival Boy went on to win the race by four lengths.

The following Saturday a high-class field of twelve runners, which included Roman Hackle (1940 winner), Poet Prince (1941 winner), Red Rower, Broken Promise and Medoc II, lined up to contest steeplechasing's most respected prize. At the last open ditch Solarium and Broken Promise were leading the field by some distance when they both fell. Red Rower, who was leading the second group, then all but fell over them. This gave Medoc II a golden opportunity which Frenchie Nicholson took. With two fences to jump Medoc II had gone into a lead of eight lengths from Red Rower, a margin that would remain as he passed the winning post. Frenchie had reversed the result of the previous Saturday and when he later rode Jack Pugh to victory in the Spa Handicap Steeplechase it completed trainer Reg Hobbs' incredible treble in one Festival Day. The only trainer to have repeated this feat since is Frenchie's son David Nicholson, when Kadı, Putty Road and Viking Flagship brought him glory in 1995.

There was no more National Hunt Racing held in England after the 1942 season until 6 January 1945 when Cheltenham held a meeting. The first race was the Rosehill Selling Hurdle Race and the winning horse was Birthlaw, owned by Major W.R. Holman (Diana Nicholson's brother) and trained by Charlie Piggott. The jockey was Frenchie Nicholson and the victory would herald not just a new dawn for the National Hunt but a sign of the success that he would achieve in this short season. By the end of the season he would be crowned joint champion jockey along with his friend Fred Rimell, each having won fifteen races.

Frenchie Nicholson going out for his last ever ride on Fairval at Wincanton, 1955.

Coincidentally the last race at that first meeting was won by Fred Rimell on Tabora in the Severn Moderate Hurdle Race.

Of his fifteen wins, Frenchie would ride three of them on Birthlaw and, remarkably, seven of them came in two days at Cheltenham in February. On the 3rd he won the Gotherington Selling Hurdle Race on Birthlaw, the Northleach Handicap Hurdle Race on Kipper Kite, the Lilley Brook Handicap Steeplechase on Fir Cone and the Ashchurch Novices' Hurdle Race (Division III) on Ursulus. Then just two weeks later on the 17th he rode three winners one after another, Jack Pugh in the Charlton Kings Handicap Steeplechase, Forestation in the Fossbridge Handicap Hurdle Race and Birthlaw in the High Class Selling Hurdle Race (Division II). He was fourth in the Gold Cup that year on Poet Prince, the winner being Red Rower – avenging his defeat of three years previously.

The following season Nicholson rode another four winners in one day, again at Cheltenham. On 10 November 1945 he saddled Karlstar in the first race of the day to win the Southam Novices' Steeplechase, then after Gene Kelly won the second division of the Cowley Novices' Steeplechase on Filum, Frenchie won the next three races: the Cheltenham Handicap Steeplechase on Poet Prince, the Dursley Handicap Hurdle Race on Quartier Maitre and the Pittville Handicap Steeplechase on Kipper Kite. All his winning rides were trained by Fulke Walwyn, the most successful trainer to send horses to Cheltenham.

The Dursley Handicap Hurdle Race at Cheltenham with Frenchie Nicholson on Quartier Maitre leading Birthlaw over the first flight, 10 November 1945. Nicholson went on to win the race, one of four wins for him on that day.

The Cheltenham Handicap Steeplechase at Cheltenham, 10 November 1945. Frenchie Nicholson nearest the camera on the Fulke Walwyn-trained Poet Prince won the race.

Frenchie Nicholson continued to ride until 1955: he rode his fourth and last Gold Cup in 1947 and in that same year won the Imperial Cup at Sandown on Tant Pis, a 20/1 outsider in a field of 33. He started training racehorses during the war at a time when he also took to farming to help the income that was so severely affected by reduced racing. He rode the winner of the 1942 Newent Handicap Steeplechase, Matador, a horse that he had trained himself, but didn't really take up training in earnest until after the war.

The first horse that Frenchie bought after getting his trainer's licence was an Irish hurdler called Mr Fitz which cost a mere £1,000. It proved a very useful acquisition as he won his first outing on 19 October 1946 when he beat Belted Monarch into second place in the Deerhurst Handicap Hurdle Race at Cheltenham with Frenchie taking the ride himself. Later in that season Frenchie rode him to success in the Liverpool Handicap Hurdle on 27 March 1947. It was a close run race with Mr Fitz just winning by a head from Caviar ridden by Archibald Jack.

At this time the Nicholsons had moved out of Lake House into Sandford Dene, but Frenchie used the stables at Lake House for his horses in training and each morning the small, but gradually increasing, string of racehorses would be taken up on to Cleeve Hill for their daily workout. As Diana came from a racing background she was quite naturally an excellent horsewoman and assisted her husband in the day-to-day running of the stables.

The best horse that Frenchie trained, certainly in the early part of his training life and possibly of his entire career, was Irish Lizard who was with him for ten years. Owned by Lord Sefton he finished third in the Grand National on two occasions, in 1953 when Early Mist took the honours and in 1954 to Royal Tan having gone to the post as a 15/2 favourite. He won three races at Cheltenham, the Tetbury Handicap Steeplechase on 11 January 1950 with Martin Molony, and the Fred Withington Handicap Steeplechase twice, in 1953 and 1954, both times jockeyed by Michael Scudamore. He also won the Topham Trophy at Aintree in 1953 with Dick Francis on board.

Another horse that brought Nicholson success was Cannobie Lee who won the Golden Miller Handicap Steeplechase at Cheltenham in three successive seasons, each time partnered by Frenchie's son David, and went on to win a total of fifteen races. It was in June 1955 that Frenchie's progress as a trainer really accelerated when Dorothy Paget, the bane of most trainers who had taken her horses, having been advised by jockey Dave Dick, started to send her horses to him. Incredibly wealthy and slightly eccentric, Miss Paget had owned such great horses as Golden Miller, Insurance, Roman Hackle and Mont Tremblant. She had won seven Gold Cups, four Champion Hurdles and a Grand National. The country's best jockeys had ridden for her and the best trainers had trained for her. Basil Briscoe, Owen Anthony and Fulke Walwyn had all taken her horses, but for one reason or another none of them maintained her patronage. Frenchie Nicholson was to be the last in a long line of trainers who would take Dorothy Paget's horses. Unfortunately the halcyon days of Golden Miller *et al.* had now passed and the horses weren't going to bring Nicholson great prizes, although he did train his fair share of Paget winners, but both the prestige of having Miss Paget as a patron and the revenue that she brought was manna from heaven.

Despite her reputation as being hard to work for, the Nicholsons coped with her eccentricities so competently that they could appreciate the qualities that were so often overlooked. During the five years that they looked after her horses she never forgot the birthdays of her jockeys and always made sure that presents were sent at Christmas for the stable lads. She was unquestionably generous and thoughtful and obviously found a good rapport with her Cheltenham trainer; nobody in the yard would hear a word against their patron.

Her eccentricities, as they were called, were that she never married, was overweight to the point of being obese in her later years, always wore the same attire when going to the races – a full-length brown overcoat and a blue beret – and gambled huge sums. She kept strange hours: she habitually slept in the day and was awake throughout the night. As a consequence she upset many of her trainers by regularly calling them in the early hours of the morning. Frenchie combated this prospective problem by refusing to have a telephone put in his bedroom; the one downstairs was perfectly adequate and it wasn't likely to waken him when in bed. A lot of these 'eccentricities' can be put down to an unloved and lonely childhood, the inheriting of great wealth when very young – she spent at least £5 million on purchasing racehorses in her lifetime. She was a diabetic and probably because of intense self-consciousness was a desperately shy woman.

Being an inveterate gambler she always wanted the best information on the horses racing against her own, so she would have her secretary ring Diana Nicholson and instruct her on what she wanted to know. Diana would then have to make a detailed inspection of the form of all the runners competing against the Paget horses and relate back her findings to the secretary. This was intense and time-consuming work, but she did it without complaint. If Diana felt there was a horse running with an outstanding chance of winning she would have to refer to this horse as a 'banco' and Miss Paget would inevitably back the horse with an outrageous gamble. The stress of knowing how much money would be risked on her opinion and how much Dorothy Paget hated losing could at times make this occupation a fraught experience, but Diana Nicholson was up to it and her ability and opinions were respected by the millionairess.

When Dorothy Paget died in February 1960 at just fifty-four years of age the Nicholson yard was immediately hit by a crisis. For five years Miss Paget had been the mainstay of a relatively small training establishment. There were just twenty-five stables at Lake House (a far cry from the ninety or so horses that David Nicholson trains today); at the peak Miss Paget was sending thirty horses to the yard. This obviously stretched resources and more lads were taken on. On her death, her executors decided to send all her horses to the May sales at Ascot, which left just six horses in training at Lake House. Nicholson was forced to cut his expenses, most of the lads had to go and for a while it was touch and go whether he would be able to continue training at all.

Despite Frenchie's success as a jockey in the 1930s and 1940s, his impact on the sport of horse racing is still very much in evidence today and ironically it is seen more clearly in the world of flat racing. As a jockey he was too heavy to be a success on the flat and by and large he trained horses to go jumping. However Nicholson had an incredible ability to bring on young apprentices to become the

Frenchie Nicholson, the trainer and arguably the best producer of apprentice jockeys that Britain has ever seen.

best jockeys in the business; some of these were National Hunt jockeys like his own son David, but the majority were to become flat-race jockeys.

Pat Eddery, Walter Swinburn and Paul Cook all came to Frenchie Nicholson's yard to learn how to become the best, and learn they did.

It was just over a year after Miss Paget died that Paul Cook was signed up as an apprentice with Frenchie. A local lad, it was his arrival at the yard that was the catalyst that moved Frenchie into the field of producing apprentices. Clearly he was a natural. Using techniques that he had picked up from his apprenticeship with Stanley Wootton as well as his own additions, Nicholson worked a hard, well-disciplined yard where all the lads had to pull their weight and adhere to strict rules. In a few short years the racing world appreciated that an apprentice coming from the Nicholson stables was to be a prized possession. They were inevitably well turned out, disciplined both in their manner and their jockeymanship and knew how to listen and take orders on riding a race. Just as Stanley Wootton had been revered as a great bringer-on of young jockeys in the early part of the century, so Frenchie was respected in the 1960s and 1970s. But more than training lads to become jockeys both Frenchie and Diana trained them for life in general. They opened bank accounts for them and taught them money management, they taught them the importance of a disciplined lifestyle and always to be polite. They organised digs for the lads in Prestbury with friendly landladies who would keep an eye on the youths. Where Stanley Wootton was an unforgiving master, Frenchie would chastise a misdemeanour and then forget the matter.

The apprenticeship of lads took on greater and greater financial importance. First they supplemented the income from training and then became the main source of income.

The successes that these jockeys enjoyed is a testament to the skill of the tutor. Paul Cook won both the St Leger and the 1000 Guineas. Pat Eddery was apprenticed in Prestbury from 1967 to 1972 and has been Champion Flat Jockey eleven times and won all the Classics save the 1000 Guineas and the Prix de l'Arc de Triomphe among a deluge of other races. Walter Swinburn joined Frenchie in 1977 and has won all the Classics apart from the St Leger at least once, and is famous for having ridden Shergar to win the 1981 Derby. In the 1982 Derby the first three finishing jockeys were all past pupils of Frenchie's. Pat Eddery won the race on Golden Fleece, Paul Cook was second on Touching Wood and Tony Murray was third on Silver Hawk.

Of the jump jockeys that he brought on, his son David has been Champion Trainer twice and is now himself a great tutor of young jockeys. Michael Dickinson saddled the first five past the post of the 1983 Gold Cup and was Champion Trainer in three successive years from 1981/2 to 1983/4. Mouse Morris rode the winner of the then Two Mile Champion Chase in successive years on Skymas and now trains very successfully back in Ireland from where he sent out Buck House to win the 1986 Queen Mother Two Mile Champion Chase. Brough Scott is a much respected television racing commentator, having had a successful riding career.

Frenchie Nicholson died on 27 April 1984 aged seventy-one, leaving behind a legacy of bright racing stars. Lest the racing world could possibly forget his great influence Cheltenham stages the Frenchie Nicholson Conditional Jockeys' Handicap Hurdle Race each October. He is buried in St Mary's churchyard in Prestbury along with his wife Diana, who died on 2 November 1997 at the age of eighty-one.

8

Richard Pitman

When he retired from being a jockey Richard Pitman wrote his autobiography and entitled it *Good Horses Make Good Jockeys*, the philosophy being that the jockey is only as good as the horse he is given to ride. This is undoubtedly true to some extent, and much of Richard Pitman's success could be put down to the fact that certainly towards the end of his riding career he was given some of the most talented horses that have ever graced the English Turf. Pendil, Crisp, Killiney, Lanzarote, Bula and Charlie Potheen all gave him the pleasure of their services.

However, for a jockey to be given the great horses he must first of all prove himself on the everyday workhorse that is unlikely to finish better than last and work himself gradually up the ladder. Richard Pitman was never the most stylish or talented of jockeys, this must be admitted, but with hard work and determination he progressed up the ladder of his chosen profession and succeeded where lesser men would have failed. From inauspicious beginnings that saw him fail to win a single race in his first four seasons, he toiled and eventually proved himself as a jockey worthy of the best mounts in England. The climb that he had to undertake to reach the top of his profession is a common one, not just in racing but in many occupations. Most top jockeys have had to toil to reach the top, but few to the extent that he had to, and therefore his achievements as a jockey must be appreciated not for the horses that he rode, but the way in which he pursued and conquered success, the determination that it took and perhaps above all the inherent love that he had for his sport that made him want to pursue his goals.

Richard Thomas Pitman was born in a Cheltenham nursing home on 21 January 1943. As a baby he lived in one of the newly built houses designed especially for the employees of Smith's Industries, which had moved from Cricklewood at the start of the war to land previously owned by Kayte Farm in Bishops Cleeve, to avoid German bombs. These new modern homes were situated in what was then known as Gay Lane and is now called Meadow Way. The Pitmans lived in one of the first of the six red-brick semi–detached houses built. Being a foreman at Smith's Industries his father, Jack, had been offered one of these new homes which he gladly took up; then as his young family grew he bought a bigger house on the Cheltenham Road, not far from Gay Lane and a mere stone's throw from the factory in which he worked. The house was named Cleevue, and being in Cheltenham Road belonged to the same stretch of road that in its recent past had been known as 'Jockeys' Row', when Billy Stott lived at Tuskar House and Tim Hamey lived at Ardeen. It was therefore fitting that

Richard Pitman spent his formative years growing up just a short distance from where two other racing heroes had lived.

As his mother was a Catholic, Richard attended St Gregory's Primary School in Cheltenham, then on passing his eleven plus he went to Tewkesbury Grammar School, where for five years he showed his academic mettle as well as his free spirit.

It was during these early years that his sister Pam was also trying to educate him – this time in the art of horsemanship. She would make him get up early each morning and cycle with him to Cleeve Hill where he would have to catch a piebald pony named Honeybunch on which to ride and learn his skills. Inevitably Honeybunch would not make it easy to be caught and the young Pitman would be exhausted even before his lessons began. At that crucial time in so many young people's lives when

A young Richard Pitman leading in Peter Doherty (brother of Phil) at Worcester.

exams dictate their future Richard Pitman was flirting with the notion of becoming a professional jockey. He sat nine O-levels and was expected to pass them all easily – his father had been so confident that he had told his friends as much. However he did exactly the opposite, belied his natural intelligence and failed them. It was perhaps one of those twists of fate that allow us to pursue a direction only because it is the only one left open to us and thus, unable to follow his father's dreams, he had to follow his own, those of becoming a jockey.

Pam was at that time seeing a young Irish jockey named Paddy Cowley – whom she later married – who was riding for the local trainer Phil Doherty in Woodmancote. From this connection the young Richard Pitman was able to secure himself a position with the trainer in 1959. Unfortunately this first job only lasted six months, ending when Phil Doherty's training licence was taken away from him after a horse in his charge was found to have a stimulant in him.

Undaunted, Richard then went for and obtained employment with Major Geoffrey Champneys in Lambourn with whom he gained his jockey's licence, but missing Cheltenham he returned to work briefly for A.A. Gilbert at Andoversford and then more substantially for John Roberts in Prestbury where he stayed for two seasons.

As a jockey his impact on the National Hunt scene in these early years was unremarkable. He failed to win a race of any kind for his first four seasons and then managed only twenty-two winners over the next three seasons. However he remained undeterred and continually worked at his riding and at realising his ambition of being a top jockey.

When it became evident that John Roberts' health was deteriorating in 1963 he started looking for yet another employer. Scouring his way through the *Horses in Training* to research the needs of trainers he discovered only that they were all well supplied with retained jockeys, stable staff and amateurs. So he then turned to looking at the jockeys riding at that time: some may have been close to retirement, wanting to go into training and therefore be looking for staff. The likes of Stan Mellor and Terry Biddlecombe didn't fit the bill as they clearly had many years left in the sport. Then it occurred to him that his boyhood hero, the masterful jockey who had guided Mandarin first past the post in the Grand Steeplechase de Paris in 1962 at Auteuil, having lost control of the horse after the third fence when the rubber bit in the horse's mouth snapped, the great Fred Winter, may be on the verge of retirement. So, with a great deal of foresight Richard Pitman wrote to the master jockey and asked to be considered if Winter ever decided to turn his hand to training. Fred replied saying that he did intend to retire at the end of the season, and he would watch Richard ride at Cheltenham. When Fred Winter had witnessed Richard Pitman's riding style over a short period he approached the young jockey, took a seat at his side, said that he thought he was an honest rider and that horses jumped for him, and most prophetically: 'You'll never be champion jockey but you'll do!'

Taking a gamble in accepting a job with an untried novice trainer, Richard Pitman made one of the most important moves in his riding career. By returning to Lambourn to work at the Uplands stables of Fred Winter for the inaugural training season of 1964/5, Richard Pitman was hardly moving up in the world. There were only five horses in training and only two other lads, Brian Delaney and Derek King. The three of them lived in a caravan whose toilet was the small wood that lay behind it!

It was Richard Pitman who rode Fred Winter's first ever runner, One Seven Seven, in the Ludlow High Sumner Challenge Cup on 21 October 1964. Unfortunately they fell at the first, but a little later on the same day Fred Winter's second runner Jay Trump won at Sandown in the Autumn Trial Chase.

The number of horses soon began to increase and by the end of the 1964/5 season the stable had won twenty-five races, but Fred Winter was largely booking outside, proven jockeys such as Stan Mellor, Dave Dick and Eddie Harty to ride his horses: Eddie Harty even joined the stables the following year as first jockey. Nevertheless Richard Pitman's first win eventually arrived when he rode Indian Spice at Fontwell Park on 30 December 1964; it had taken him over four years and sixty attempts to achieve a winner. It was a turning point, not a huge one, but a small sign of greater things to come. He had two other winners that season and they both came on 19 April at Towcester: Savonarola in the Hulcote Handicap Steeplechase and Minute Gun in the Felix Fenston Challenge Cup, both horses owned and trained by Bill Shand-Kydd.

Talking to the Guv'nor, Fred Winter, during a morning's schooling session.

Uplands, and Fred Winter leading out. On the horse behind is John Francome; Richard Pitman is wearing the jacket and cloth cap.

The following season he began to pick up more spare rides and his tally of winners doubled. It included his first win at Cheltenham in the Ernest Robinson Handicap Hurdle Race on 1 January 1966 on Minute Gun and his first major win on 19 March 1966, when he won the Imperial Cup at Sandown on Royal Sanction.

At the beginning of the season, on 2 October 1965, Richard Pitman married a Leicestershire farmer's daughter, the beautiful blonde Jenny Harvey, on whom he had first set eyes in Cheltenham. He was still working for John Roberts at that time and she was riding out for Chris Taylor in Bishops Cleeve. They would have two sons together, Mark Andrew and Paul Richard, and many years later Jenny Pitman would become the first lady trainer of a Grand National winner: Corbiere in 1983 and then Royal Athlete in 1995, and the first lady to train the winner of the Gold Cup: Burrough Hill Lad in 1984 and then Garrison Savannah in 1991.

The following season, 1966/7, Richard Pitman was offered the position of first jockey by Major Verly Bewicke, which he took while still remaining crucially at the Fred Winter yard. He began to ride much more regularly, although the number of winners didn't increase by the same ratio. As well as the number of rides, the quality of the horses was improving, which was putting him in the frame and thus in the eye of other trainers. On Saturday 8 April 1967 Richard Pitman was given his first mount in the Grand National, on Dorimont for Bill Shand-Kydd. It was the year of the multiple pile-up at the twenty-third fence when the riderless Popham Down ran straight across the front of the jump. It was total chaos and Pitman's mount fell along with many others. Only the eventual 100/1 winner Foinavon ridden by John Buckingham jumped the fence first time.

The National of the following year saw Richard ride Fred Winter's Manifest into eleventh place and then in the 1968/9 season, his ninth as a professional jockey and to that date having accumulated a tally of just forty-four winners, he really turned the tide. The National on 29 March saw him bring Steel Bridge second past the post, twelve lengths behind Eddie Harty on Highland Wedding, and for the first time in his career he got into the winning jockeys' table – in twelfth position by winning 33 of his races from 188 mounts, a success rate of 17.6 per cent. This compares very favourably to the performance of the champion jockey of that season, Terry Biddlecombe, who won 77 from 372 rides – a success rate of only 20.7 per cent.

At the start of the following season Fred Winter's first jockey, Bobby Beasley, retired and Fred Winter looked to the man who had stuck with him for so long to become his replacement. He turned it down as he was still contracted to Major Bewicke, and the position instead went to Paul Kelleway, with Richard Pitman remaining as second jockey. Nevertheless it was a Winter-trained horse that gave him the John Smith's Yorkshire Handicap Steeplechase on 24 January 1970 at Doncaster – Freddie Boy owned by Mrs Vestey. Freddie Boy then went on to give Pitman his first ride in the Cheltenham Gold Cup on 19 March of that year when they finished fourth in a race won for the first time by L'Escargot.

On 25 April Tim Handel booked him to ride Royal Toss at Sandown in the Whitbread Gold Cup; they started the race at odds of 20/1 and finished six lengths clear of second-placed Charter Flight. At the end of the season he had ridden one more winner than the previous year and at this time he ended his association with Major Bewicke, leaving him free to share the first jockey position in the Winter yard with Paul Kelleway, a position that he wouldn't hold on his own until 1972/3 when John Francome was named as his second. It was to be the start of five great seasons in which he would gradually increase his tally of winners and become associated with some of the greatest horses ever to have graced National Hunt. But it wasn't just Winter-trained horses that Richard Pitman guided to success during these halcyon days. It was for Fulke Walwyn, Fred Winter's neighbour and rival, that Richard Pitman won the Hennessy Cognac Gold Cup Handicap Steeplechase at Newbury on 25 November 1972 on Charlie Potheen.

The 1973 Cheltenham Festival expected great things from Fred Winter's stable. He had at that time arguably the best five horses in training and only Lanzarote of those five was not going to make the trip. However, of the remaining four, Crisp would finish third to Inkslinger in the National Hunt Two Mile Champion Chase, Bula (the only one of the four not to be ridden by Pitman – instead he was jockeyed by Paul Kelleway) finished a very disappointing fifth to the Fred Rimell-trained Comedy of Errors in the Champion Hurdle and Pendil failed by a small head in the Gold Cup. Only Killiney would meet the expectations put on them and that was in the Totalisator Champion Steeplechase, winning by an impressive five lengths from Bountiful Charles. Killiney was a giant of a horse at 17.1 hands on which Richard Pitman finished second in the Bingley Novices' Hurdle Race (Division 3) at Ascot on 20 November 1970. They then went on to win the next five races of that season. Eddie Harty and Paul Kelleway rode the horse in the last two races of the season, before Pitman regained the ride in a disappointing 1971/2 season when the horse only ran twice, with a second place as the best result, but then in the 1972/3 season the horse and his jockey set the racing world alight. Never separated, they won eight races from eight starts, which included that wonderful Festival win. Tragedy struck however at Ascot on Saturday 7 April, when going off at 4/9 odds-on favourite in the Heinz Steeplechase, Killiney, the horse that had been nicknamed the 'Gentle Giant' and who had shown such incredible talent, fell badly at the ninth and had to be humanely destroyed.

Another of Fred Winter's great racing stars was Bula who, with Paul Kelleway up won the Champion Hurdle in 1971 and 1972, but when they failed so badly in the 1973 race Pitman took over the ride for the Welsh Champion Hurdle of that year and improved on the position, but still only managed to finish second, four lengths behind Comedy of Errors. The following season Pitman and Bula then went on to win their first four races together which included the Black and White Whisky Gold Cup at Ascot in November. The partnership ended after they fell at Sandown in February 1974 and the upcoming jockey John Francome took over the ride on the ageing maestro.

The horse that brought Richard Pitman the greatest number of big races was Pendil. It was this horse that won him his first of five Festival races when together they won the Arkle Challenge Trophy on 15 March 1972. Richard Pitman didn't have to wait very long to take his second Festival race; it came the very next day in

Richard Pitman on Killiney, the 'Gentle Giant' that won the 1973 Sun Alliance Steeplechase. (Courtesy of Bernard Parkin)

Richard Pitman and Pendil going to the post for the 1974 Cheltenham Gold Cup. (Courtesy of Bernard Parkin)

the Cathcart Challenge Cup when he was partnering Soloning. Pendil and Pitman had already won at Cheltenham, on 10 December 1971 in the Bath Novices' Steeplechase, but it would be the following season that really brought the spotlight on to the partnership. Starting with the Black and White Whisky Gold Cup at Ascot on 18 November, they won five of their six races for the season, picking up the King George VI Chase in the process, and only failing to make it six out of six by the shortest of heads.

That sixth race of the 1972/3 season was the Cheltenham Gold Cup and Pendil went off as 4/6 favourite. The tactics of the race were discussed at great length beforehand by Richard Pitman and Fred Winter. They both knew and agreed that Pendil raced best when he had a horse to race against (in so many of his victories there had not been the class of horse to trouble him anyway), but in the Gold Cup there would be, and so Richard Pitman really wanted to hold him back from the lead until after the last fence. Fred Winter concurred that usually this was the soundest approach, but he was nervous that if Pendil jumped badly at that last he would not be able to get back into the race; if he was leading and jumped badly there might still be the space to win. Throughout the race Pendil jumped superbly, and with Terry Biddlecombe on Charlie Potheen in front the horse was perfectly placed. As they came to turn for home Charlie Potheen began to slow and Richard Pitman eased his horse past him and into the lead. Second from last Pendil was three lengths clear of The Dikler in second place, and he was still jumping superbly. Then as they were halfway up the run-in Pendil lost concentration and he started to falter, the horse had nothing in front of him to run against and the sudden noise and colour of the crowds momentarily took his attention. Ron Barry on The Dikler drove past and headed for glory. Pitman worked away at his charge and they began to fight back showing the spirit of true champions, but it was too late and The Dikler took the title by a short head.

The following season was another tale of success and failure, four out of the partnership's five rides were victories. Among them were the Massey-Ferguson Gold Cup at Cheltenham on 8 December 1973 and their second King George VI Chase in succession at Kempton Park on Boxing Day as usual. The defeat was once more in the Cheltenham Gold Cup. Richard Pitman approached the race brimming with confidence: like the punters who backed him down to an 8/13 odds-on favourite, he could see nothing in the race that would stop them. However, a sure thing in horseracing is often the kiss of death and unbeknownst to Richard Pitman this was exactly what Fred Winter and Vince Brookes, Pendil's lad, were afraid of. For Fred Winter had received a threat by someone claiming to be the IRA that Pendil would be shot during the Gold Cup. Fred told only Vince Brookes who subsequently slept in with the horse at night. Richard Pitman was left in blissful ignorance of the threat until the paddock before the big race. Noticing that Vince Brookes was looking unwell he asked why, and it was then that the stable lad told Pitman of the threat and pleaded for the jockey to pull Pendil out of the race rather than risk the horse's life. Of course he couldn't do that and he left for the start of the race ashen faced.

Throughout the race Pendil looked in impressive form, jumping well and positioned to attack when necessary; then at the twentieth High Ken fell right in

Crisp winning at Doncaster in the Doncaster Pattern Chase, 10 November 1973. Trailing in eight lengths behind is Red Rum.

front of him. Both Pendil and Pitman went down as if shot by an assassin's bullet. Spectating, the poor Vince Brookes was convinced that his beloved charge was dead; then when both jockey and horse got up safely any possible disappointment there might have been that they hadn't won the race was forgotten by a wave of relief that the horse hadn't been shot. The following season Pendil and Richard Pitman recommenced their winning ways with their first race of the season together on 26 October 1974 at Newbury by taking the Hermitage Chase, a week later they won the Sandown Handicap Pattern Chase and then at Haydock the Sundew Chase on 27 November. Trying to win the King George VI Chase for a third successive year they were undone by a mistake at the fifteenth, which gave Captain Christy room to record an eight-length victory over them. They were almost pushed into third by Soothsayer who was being driven all the way by John Francome, but Pendil clung on to take second place by three-quarters of a length. He didn't make it to the Festival for that year: after another second place in the Newbury Spring Handicap Chase he finished lame in third place for the Yellow Pages Pattern Handicap Chase at Kempton Park in February. For over a year Pendil would be sidelined, and by the time he was fit again Richard Pitman had moved on to other ambitions.

On 11 March 1971 Richard Pitman rode Crisp in the horse's first race on British soil, having been brought over from Australia where he was a champion chaser. It was at Wincanton in the Broadstone Handicap Steeplechase and they won it by fifteen lengths in a then record time of 3 minutes 55 seconds. Crisp would later give Richard Pitman his second race in the Gold Cup when they finished fifth to Glencaraig Lady on 16 March 1972 and then most famously of all the 1973 Grand National. Starting the race as a 9/1 joint favourite with Red Rum, Crisp immediately took control and gave a jumping performance unequalled in the race's history. By the start of the second circuit Crisp and his jockey were twenty-five lengths clear of the pack and oozing class. At the last Becher's they were twenty lengths clear and looking uncatchable, but Brian Fletcher, on that Aintree phenomenon Red Rum who was in the race for the first time, had different ideas. Slowly they began to eat up the Australian horse's lead. The incredible pace that the big horse had set began to tell and as he came to the elbow he was clearly suffering fatigue; nevertheless his heart didn't give out and with 100 yards to go they were still six lengths clear, but then in the last few strides the race was lost as Red Rum eased past the post three-quarters of a length ahead of Crisp and Richard Pitman. The race, although Red Rum's in victory and the first of his incredible five Nationals when he won three and was runner-up twice, is still often referred to as Crisp's National, and if ever a horse and its jockey had deserved to win the race Crisp and Richard Pitman were that pair. In beating Crisp, Red Rum had set a new race record of 9 minutes 1.9 seconds, a full 19 seconds faster than the previous record held by Golden Miller and set in 1934, thirty-nine years previously. And what must not be overlooked is that Crisp was giving away a staggering 23 lb in weight to Red Rum.

Although Richard Pitman was not the type of jockey to rue his luck – he rode out of pleasure rather than self-aggrandisement – this second second placing in the sport's major events in the space of just sixteen days (the other being Pendil's failure in the Gold Cup) must surely have made his heart ache just a little. Both Pendil and Crisp had looked set to win their races and lost them in the last strides.

On 10 November that same year Crisp and Red Rum faced each other again in the Doncaster Pattern Chase over three miles and two furlongs. There were no other runners and the horses were both carrying 11 stone 10 lb. Crisp and Richard Pitman won the race by eight lengths.

The 1974 Festival was one that Richard Pitman can look back on with great pride. Although failing to win the Gold Cup he finished second in the Sun Alliance Novices' Hurdle Race on the first day when Ron Barry on Brown Lad beat his mount, Rely, and he won the last race of the meeting, the Cathcart Challenge Cup on Soothsayer – a horse with which he would finish second in the following year's Gold Cup. However, to cap it all the horse that he won the Imperial Cup with when run at Kempton Park and not Sandown the previous March, Lanzarote, brought him the biggest success of his career, the Champion Hurdle.

Lanzarote and Richard Pitman first raced together on 27 January 1973 at Kempton Park after the horse had won one race with Paul Kelleway and then been unsuccessfully ridden by Vic Soane and a young John Francome. That first race with Pitman, the Ladbroke Handicap Hurdle Race, they won by ten lengths. They then won the rest of the races that season, which included the Imperial Cup (mentioned above), and went the next season unbeaten in all of their six races together. It was

Richard Pitman on Crisp in the Parade of Champions at The Horse of The Year Show, Wembley, 1975.

The last fence in his last race, riding St Swithin to finish sixth at Stratford in the Whipcord Chase, 31 May 1975.

only in Richard Pitman's last season in the saddle, 1974/5, that they showed any vulnerability, winning a comparatively paltry four out of nine races. Among those winners was the Welsh Champion Hurdle on 1 April 1975. Of the five defeats, three of them were to Fred Rimell's twice Champion Hurdle winner, Comedy of Errors.

In 1973 the BBC had approached Richard Pitman to offer him the job as a paddock man for both their flat and jump racing coverage. With the Winter stables full of talent and prospective winners he turned the job down gracefully. Then in 1975 they repeated the offer. At this time the young jockey that he had helped to nurture and guide, John Francome, was sharing the rides at the stables. Talking it over with Fred Winter, he was told that for as long as he wanted there was a job for him at Uplands. Richard Pitman then asked Fred Winter if he would ever run Pendil in the Grand National. Winter said no as the horse's legs were not good enough. With that announcement his mind was made up, and he retired from racing to become a broadcaster. He first covered the Cheltenham Festival in 1976.

In retiring from the saddle he made true Fred Winter's prophetic words, he had indeed been good enough to win races but he never did win the champion jockey title. Twice he was runner-up, both times to Ron Barry, in 1972/3 and 1973/4 when he rode 84 and 79 wins respectively. In his fifteen-season career he saddled a total of 430 winners, which, considering that for the first seven he only managed a total of 22 winners, is an impressive record.

In 1977 his marriage with Jenny broke down and they were divorced. In 1979 he remarried. His beautiful bride was Mandy Jefferies, and John Francome acted

Richard Pitman's marriage to Mandy Jefferies in 1979. John Francome stands on the right as his best man.

Richard Pitman with some of the horses at his yard shortly after retiring from race riding.

as his best man, duplicating the role that Richard had played at his wedding. After retiring from racing Richard Pitman started his own bloodstock company with some considerable success. One mare in particular, Cuckoo Flower, was the mother of winners of 27 races. Her first winner was Foxy Games sired by New Member, Edelweiss kept up the tradition and Mugoni Beach who went to be trained with Martin Pipe, with victories on the flat and in National Hunt, confirmed the pedigree of Cuckoo Flower.

The proudest and happiest moment in Richard Pitman's broadcasting career happened on Gold Cup Day in 1991 when he reported the victory of Garrison Savannah, trained by Jenny Pitman and owned by Cheltenham-based Autofour Engineering. In the saddle was his son Mark. The famous exuberant clenched-fist salute by Mark on this occasion was for his father, sitting up in the commentary box.

While breaking in a difficult yearling in 1992 Richard Pitman suffered a horrific accident that could conceivably have cost his life. He was thrown from the horse and winded, and the yearling then attacked him, causing considerable injury to his head. The following day his head had blown up like a football and he started to suffer double vision. He was rushed to hospital, but the build-up of pressure in his head and hence on the optic nerve and the interference of floating bone fragments in his skull ultimately lost him the use of one eye.

He now lives in a small village in Oxfordshire with his wife and their two daughters, and supplements his income from broadcasting and journalism by writing non-fiction racing books and more recently some excellent racing thrillers, in which the hero is Eddie Malloy, a tough, honest jockey with a bent for righting injustices.

Richard Pitman was and is the epitome of what a jockey should be – hardworking, brave and most of all in love with the sport. He genuinely loved to ride and loved to jump. He considers himself incredibly fortunate to have earned a living from the sport that he loves most of all, and blessed to have ridden the horses that he did. There is no bitterness about the failures or what was so nearly his, just gratitude that he has been allowed to do what he has done. If only more could be so.

9

Paul Cook

When Paul Cook won the 1982 St Leger on Touching Wood it was the affirmation that a jockey who had shown such natural ability and promise as an aspiring apprentice could, with determination and hard work, put behind him the disappointments of not building immediately on that promise and yet achieve the results owed to him. Paul Cook had been in the racing wilderness for too long when he won that race and yet he had stuck it out, worked hard at getting rides and at his riding and, as had been his characteristic all his life, shown determination to achieve something that lesser men would have given up as lost.

Paul Allan Cook was born in Cheltenham on 12 April 1946, the son of Alice Dorothy and George Cook. His father held a variety of jobs at different times, including working on a market, as a hospital nurse, as an employee of the Whitbread Brewery in Cheltenham and as a landworker. The family never had much money and there were few luxuries to be shared in the childhood home of Paul and his brother Philip George Cook. Living in Alstone Lane he went to Elmfield and Arle Road schools in Cheltenham, and to all intents and purposes a career in horseracing seemed the unlikeliest of results for a boy brought up in one of Cheltenham's newest council estates.

However, while Paul was still at school a butcher friend named Frederick Jones suggested to the small, ginger-haired, quiet and unassuming fourteen-year-old that he write to Frenchie Nicholson in Prestbury to see if he had any vacancies to work in his stables. This was the time before telephones were ubiquitous and for a young lad to find an address or a telephone number for somebody working the other side of the town was no easy matter. Nevertheless, eventually the young boy managed to get an address. He put pen to paper and wrote to Frenchie Nicholson for a job, never yet having sat upon a horse. In due course word came back to Paul that there weren't any vacancies at the stables, but if he wanted to help out during the school holidays he was most welcome.

Young Paul jumped at the chance, and at weekends and holidays he would jump on his bicycle, pedal his way to the stables and help with any chores that needed to be done. He was very keen to do well and worked so hard that both Frenchie and Diana took a great liking to the lad and started giving him a few shillings a week to follow the bigger apprentices around the yard with a grease pot. After about a year of menial, routine labour, Paul had grown enough for the Nicholsons to consider putting him on the back of their daughter Josie's pony. It would be his first experience of being on a horse and one which he was

Elmfield School in Cheltenham, which Paul Cook attended as a junior.

determined to get used to. Soon he had graduated to the point of riding Desert Fort, an aged steeplechaser still resident in the Nicholson yard, on the way back from the stable's string workout on the Cleeve Hill Downs.

Five days after he had celebrated his fifteenth birthday, on 17 April 1961, Paul Cook signed apprenticeship papers with Frenchie Nicholson and in so doing cemented the destinies of both individuals. For Frenchie it would be the first in a very long and illustrious line of apprentices that would enter his 'academy', be nurtured and leave to attain great heights; for Cook it was the start of a tremendous five-year apprenticeship that would lead to a lifelong career associated with horses.

Much to his chagrin, it was David Nicholson, Frenchie's son, who was to school Paul into being able to ride a horse properly. After a long hard week he had to take the apprentice on Sundays and teach him the techniques that he had known virtually since birth. It was a hard task for Nicholson junior as Cook had none of the natural knowledge or technique that he had had instilled into him by generations of horse handlers. It seemed to take Paul an age to even grasp the basics of riding, but the lad was enthusiastic and very determined, and eventually was competent enough to be allowed to take some of the less troublesome horses in the yard out for their workouts.

A sign of Frenchie's commitment and belief in the lad came when he bought two horses specifically with Paul Cook in mind to ride them. One was named Tenor, the other Balle d'Or, and it was the latter that gave Cook his debut in racing when in July 1962 he rode him at Bath.

At this stage of his career there was still a good deal of scepticism among the Nicholsons as to whether Cook would ever make the grade as a jockey. When he rode, Diana Nicholson would later recall, he would begin to take on the appearance of a frog. His hands would gradually move further and further forward up the horse's neck and his legs would move correspondingly further and further behind him so that he was almost horizontal over the horse's back. Yet Diana Nicholson would also say that horses ran for Paul, and so to try and improve his riding and get him to use his legs better, Diana offered the lad 2s 6d for every horse that finished behind him when he was to ride Tenor in a race at Warwick. To some degree the financial incentive worked and when Tenor and Cook finished in front of two horses he earned himself 5s.

It was Diana Nicholson's job to ferry the apprentice around from racecourse to racecourse as Frenchie was too busy training the jumping prospects in his stables, and it was while she was doing this for Paul Cook that she had the idea that training flat racing apprentices could be a good sideline for the Nicholsons. After running the idea past Frenchie they agreed to have a go, with Frenchie doing the training of the apprentices and Diana running the business. As a consequence of Paul Cook's apprentice success the success of many others like Pat Eddery and Tony Murray was determined.

Nevertheless there was still plenty of work to do on Cook and a lot of learning for the apprentice to do, and he went about it always with enthusiasm and determination to succeed. Another hard lesson came after Frenchie laid into him for over-using the whip during a race at Bath, and as a punishment the trainer banned the lad from using the whip at all for a month. Despite the rigours of working and being apprenticed with the Nicholsons, Paul Cook still remembers this time with affection, and although Frenchie Nicholson was strict and demanding, he maintains that he was always fair both in praise and criticism.

In September 1963 Cook finally got his first win under his belt when, riding in a race at Warwick, he was beaten by a short head by Joe Mercer. The result of the race was taken to the stewards with the complaint being that Mercer was guilty of bumping. After due consideration the stewards found against Mercer and Cook won the race in the stewards' room.

With that first win interest in the apprentice began to increase and offers of rides began to filter in. Then after a two-mile handicap race at Newbury in which he saw Cook finish fifth, Paddy Prendergast was sufficiently impressed by the riding display that he booked him to ride Credo in the 1964 Chester Cup. Before the race the trainer gave the apprentice strict instructions on how to tackle the race and the jockey carried them out almost to the letter. He held Credo back just long enough to strike out fast and late and won the race in a photo-finish from Scobie Breasley on Utrillo.

The young apprentice really began to become known and was in huge demand. He finished the 1964 season as champion apprentice with 46 winners and at the start of the 1965 season Paddy Prendergast took out first claim on his services in England and for the Irish Classics. Diana Nicholson later stated that the youth was so popular and in such demand that it felt at times as though they were managing the fifth Beatle, and yet he was never in any rush to leave the Prestbury stables for greener pastures. Wisely he appreciated the importance of staying with the Nicholsons and would ultimately see out all five years of his apprenticeship with them.

Again in 1965 he finished the season as champion apprentice, this time with 62 winners, chalking up his first century of winners in August 1965 in a then-record time of under two years. When he turned professional in 1966 it seemed inevitable that his rise up the professional jockeys' table would be just as successful.

He was snatched up by Sir Jack Jarvis in Newmarket to be the trainer's first jockey with Bruce Hobbs taking out a second claim on his services, and he did manage a few very impressive wins. The season started fantastically with a fabulous display of riding at the Guineas Meeting at Newmarket in April. Over the three days he was booked for sixteen rides: the first of these on 26 April was Camisole in the Littleport Stakes with which he finished sixth, Bivouac in the Totalisator Spring Handicap finished seventh and then he recorded a third with St Puckle in the Jockey Club Stakes; another third in the Ely Handicap on Tiger Hunt and then he won the Hastings Maiden Stakes on Welsh Dee. The following day, the day of the 2000 Guineas, he won the Botesdale Handicap on Sandray before putting in a good performance in the first Classic of the season on Pretendre. Looking good and with an even chance two furlongs out Pretendre couldn't quicken and ended up eighth of the twenty-five runners, with Jimmy Lindley on Kashmir II taking the honours. It was nevertheless a good effort by both horse and jockey and a pointer to future events.

The last day of Newmarket was a day for the young jockey to savour. He brought Nellie home in third place in the Wilbraham Maiden Stakes, after which he was coupled with the Vincent O'Brien-trained and Mrs Alice Mills-owned Glad Rags for the 1000 Guineas. A small filly at just fifteen hands and three inches high she was a determined creature that needed careful handling. That is exactly what Paul Cook did. At the age of just twenty, Cook nursed the 100/6 chance Glad Rags round the course, carefully monitoring Berkeley Springs who to all intents and purposes appeared to have won the race ever since she had taken up the running at the Bushes. Then coming into the Dip it was Cook on Glad Rags who was first in pursuing Berkeley Springs and coming up the hill his horse reeled the other in and they took the race on the line by a head. Two lengths behind in third was the 11/10 on French favourite Miliza II. The very next race, the Culford Maiden Stakes, Paul Cook was riding for Jack Jarvis on the Lord Rosebery-owned Snob, and duly won it. With three wins over the three days, one being a Classic, it certainly appeared that Paul Cook was starting his professional career in the same vein that he had left his apprenticeship.

Later in the year he would notch up other notable wins. For H. Blagrave he won the Jubilee Handicap at Kempton Park on Antiquarian and for his employer Sir Jack Jarvis he took the Chester Vase on General Gordon and the King Edward VII Stakes at Royal Ascot on Pretendre – the horse he had ridden in the 2000 Guineas and which he would come so desperately close to winning the Epsom Derby with in his very first year as a professional. That Derby was run on 25 May 1966, and Pretendre was joint favourite with Lester Piggott's mount Right Noble at 9/2. The start was delayed for fifteen minutes because Charlottown needed to be reshod, but then an epic encounter was under way. It was Right Noble that was in the lead coming round Tattenham Corner, but halfway up the straight it was well beaten with Paul Cook fighting out the finish coming up the hill with the 52-year-old Australian Scobie Breasley. Breasley took the race by a neck on the line with Charlottown, his second win in the race in three years and the first English triumph for five years. Nevertheless, praise for Cook's riding was all around the course, particularly from Sir Jack Jarvis who had been confident in Pretendre taking the race.

Ostensibly things seemed to be going perfectly for Paul Cook, but the hectic life of Newmarket compared to Cheltenham took a lot of getting used to and he was not totally comfortable with his change in lifestyle. The following year, 1967, his second with Sir Jack Jarvis, he took the Chester Cup on Mahbub Aly for W.R. Hern, but things gradually got worse and by the end of the season he lost his job with the Newmarket trainer.

He went freelance in 1968, an incredibly difficult way of ensuring enough rides, let alone good prospective winning rides, for any jockey to pay all the bills, and his fortunes fell dramatically. When the winners stopped coming the fickle crowds who had bayed him home soon forgot him. It would be through sheer hard work and determination, taking rides in eleven different countries, that would eventually bring him back to his rightful position.

With agents today taking such a controlling interest in jockeys' affairs and making it their business to keep their clients employed, the life of a freelance jockey is probably less pressured than it was thirty years ago – they can concentrate more on riding to their best ability and perhaps leave the worry of where the next ride is coming from to their agent. Paul Cook had no such luxury: without a retainer guaranteeing rides and the kudos of being a retained jockey life became very tough, and he was left in the doldrums of the racing world for several years. Even by taking some rides abroad it wouldn't be until 1972 that he won a really major race, but in the same spirit that he entered the world of racing – with grit, determination and a quiet enthusiasm to succeed – he persevered and finally proved his worth as a top flat-race jockey.

While still in the employ of Sir Jack Jarvis, in 1967 Paul Cook met a young, beautiful girl back in his home town of Cheltenham called Carol Anne. Two years later on 4 February 1969, after a disastrous racing season, he and Carol Anne married in the most romantic of settings, Malibu Hill in Bombay, India. Through the hardest years of his racing career Carol Anne would remain and support Paul Cook, and with the birth of their two sons and a daughter there was always a family to maintain the jockey's faith in his own ability.

After four barren years, it was Bruce Hobbs who gave him the ride on Touch Paper to win the Stewards' Cup at Goodwood in 1972, and the following year Cook took the same race again, this time on Michael Stoute's horse Alphadamus. They were chinks of light in an otherwise dark period.

Two years later however there were more and better results being had: the 1975 Diomed Stakes at Epsom was won by Paul Cook on All Friends, trained by the Lambourn trainer Nicholas Vigors, as was the July Stakes at Newmarket of the

Paul Cook up on Lorelene, his third placed mount in the 1979 Cesarewitch at Newmarket. (Courtesy of Bernard Parkin)

same year with the G. Hunter-trained Super Cavalier. The following year All Friends once again did the work for Cook in the Diomed Stakes and a horse that he would have a good relationship with, Gentilhombre, brought him home first at Royal Ascot in the Cork and Orrery Stakes.

By the latter half of the 1970s, Paul Cook had really managed to turn his career back on course as he started to reel in victory after victory in the important races. In 1977 he had victories in the Jersey Stakes at Royal Ascot with the Michael Stoute-trained Etienne Gerard; the July Cup at Newmarket, the Diadem Stakes at Ascot and the one kilometre long Prix de l'Abbaye de Longchamp in France all gave him wins on Gentilhombre. The following year he won the Mill Reef Stakes at Newbury on King of Spain for trainer Peter Cundell, and then the Ebor Handicap at York on Totowah. By the end of the 1978 season he had ridden more winners than ever before, totalling 90.

Michael Stoute in 1979 gave him the winning rides for all three of his major wins, the July Stakes at Newmarket and the Doncaster Champagne Stakes, both on Final Straw, and the Richmond Stakes at Goodwood on Castle Green. In 1980 Cook added the Lancashire Oaks run at Haydock Park to his ever-increasing tally with the Bruce Hobbs-trained Vielle, and once again finished the season with 90 winners, a tally equalling that of 1978 and which he ultimately wouldn't better.

The following year it looked as though Paul Cook was carrying on where he had left off, and although he would finish the season with only 84 winning rides

Paul Cook on Russian George in the Bessborough Stakes at Royal Ascot in June 1981 on the day that he completed a double. (Courtesy of Bernard Parkin)

The second part of Cook's double. He is seen here on Fly Baby, having won the Queen Mary Stakes. (Courtesy of Bernard Parkin)

he had one weekend at the beginning of July that resulted in his racing achievements getting him into the record books. On Friday 3 July he started a memorable winning sequence of rides at Haydock in the afternoon when his mount, Norwick, won the prestigious Cock of the North Stakes by beating just one other horse. The jockey then went on to the evening meeting at Beverley where he took the first two races on the card, first aboard Goldliner Abbey and then on Chester County. To follow this treble he went on to score another treble the following day, American Independence Day, but incredibly at different meetings. This feat started at Sandown Park where he won the Anniversary Handicap by three-quarters of a length on Prince's Gate. He then took a helicopter to Bath where he rode Ramannolie in the Southmead Stakes and won by just a head. Airborne again he flew to Nottingham and put in an impressive riding exhibition to thrust Pavilion to win the Notts County Football Club Handicap by a head. To add to these six winners in two days at five different courses, Paul Cook also won a double at Royal Ascot on 17 June: the Queen Mary Stakes on Fly Baby and the Bessborough Stakes on Russian George. Then once again riding Peter Cundell's King of Spain he won the King George Stakes at Goodwood.

He was still chalking up the big races in 1982 when he was given the best horse of his career to ride, Touching Wood owned by Sheikh Maktoum Al Maktoum and trained by Harry Thomson Jones in Newmarket. On Wednesday 2 June Pat Eddery won the two hundred and third Epsom Derby in the fastest time for 46 years on Golden Fleece, the son of the 1970 Triple Crown winner Nijinsky. Three lengths behind, finishing in second place for the second time in his career for the race, was Paul Cook on the 40/1 shot Touching Wood; one length behind him was Silver Hawk, ridden by Tony Murray. Remarkably all three placed riders were past pupils of Frenchie Nicholson.

Just over three months later, on 11 September, Cook proved beyond all doubt that his resurgence as a top flat race jockey was complete by winning the St Leger at Doncaster by a margin of one and half lengths on Touching Wood. Starting as a 7/1 shot it took courage and stamina by the horse and knowledge and determination by the jockey to win this one and three-quarter-mile race for three-year-olds. The race was an epic battle between Touching Wood and Zilos, with Zilos partnered by Geoff Baxter looking as though he would power his way past Touching Wood coming to the finish, but Paul Cook got his mount to find an extra gear from somewhere and with a half a furlong to go went clear. Touching Wood also gave Cook his first and only victory in the Irish St Leger at The Curragh that same year.

Things could hardly get better for the jockey who was now aged thirty-six, and so he began to look around for a business with a view to his ultimate retirement from riding. In 1983 he found such an opportunity, and without intending to retire immediately, he bought Meadow Farm Stud at Ramsbury in Wiltshire to build up and develop for his post-riding future. It would be a further six years before he would finally hang up his jockey silks, and in the interim years he added a third Diomed Stakes to his collection when he rode Lofty for H.T. Jones in 1983, a second Ebor Handicap when the Cornelius Horgan-trained Western Dancer came home in 1985, and the following year on the same horse he took the

Paul Cook up on Lyphards' Special in the Champion Stakes at Newmarket, October 1983. (Courtesy of Bernard Parkin)

Chester Cup, a race he had only previously won back in 1967. In 1987 he won the race formerly known as the Royal Stakes at Sandown, the Guardian Classic Trial, on the Paul Kelleway-trained Gulf King; over in Rome he won the Premio Parioli on the Ian Balding-trained and Mrs J. A. McDougald-owned Lucratif, to prove that he could truly ride winners anywhere.

Paul Cook's career came to a slightly premature end in 1989 after a nasty accident at Doncaster in which the horse that he was riding put his foot in a hole on the course and fell, throwing and injuring his jockey. Paul Cook had however been a professional jockey for over twenty years, and although his retirement from the saddle was enforced, it wouldn't have been a career that he would have wished to sustain for much longer. He turned instead to concentrate on the stud that he had been building up for the past six years, with his wife acting as the manager. They had already bred the very successful Our Dynasty and went on to have success both at home and abroad with such horses as Brocklesby and Misterioso – the latter of which they bought as a foal and retained, winning with it the Blue Seal at Ascot and the Rockingham Stakes at York.

Paul Cook's daughter Aimee Virginia has now followed in her father's footsteps, and until he retired at the end of the 1998 season she rode as an apprentice to the Queen's trainer, Lord Huntingdon.

10

Jim Wilson

Arguably the best amateur jockey of his day, Andrew James Wilson was born on 4 February 1950 in Maidstone, Kent, to a well-known racing family. His maternal grandfather was Colonel T.R. Pearson, his great-aunt was Mrs D. Beddington whose horse Kirriemuir won the 1965 Champion Hurdle ridden by G.W. Robinson and trained by Fulke Walwyn, his mother's sister Diana married Fred Winter, and his mother owned the wonderful Herring Gull, winner of the 1968 Totalisator Champion Novices' Steeplechase at Cheltenham with John Crowley in the saddle and the first Cheltenham winner for Paddy Mullins. Another aunt, Mrs Bobbie Gundry, would own Little Owl, the horse with which he would become synonymous.

In 1969, on the recommendation of his uncle Fred Winter, Jim Wilson arrived at David Nicholson's stables at Condicote to start an apprenticeship. Then as now, David Nicholson ran a tight and disciplined ship much in the style of his father Frenchie, and it was Fred Winter's belief that if anyone could control the slightly wayward young jockey, David Nicholson would be the one. The dress code and smart appearance of all apprentices, amateurs and conditional jockeys had always been strictly maintained, so when Jim Wilson turned up with his long hair he was told in no uncertain terms to have it cut. When he was a bit lax in carrying out the operation, electric clippers were produced and the issue was immediately sorted out.

To this day David Nicholson recollects the problems of being able to control the free-spirited Wilson who came in at all hours of the day and night, and if quizzed as to what he had eaten recently he would often reply, 'Ah Jesus, sex, cheese and water biscuits'. Nevertheless as with so many other jockeys since, much of Jim Wilson's later success in the saddle can be put down to the foundations implemented at Condicote with 'The Duke'.

At Lower Swell, near Stow-on-the-Wold on 6 September 1975 Jim Wilson married David Nicholson's secretary, Melinda Jane Carden, and in so doing enhanced his racing heritage, becoming the son-in-law of 'Boy' Pilkington and his wife Jane. For an income Wilson had taken on an equine swimming pool business based at his home at Glenfall Stables, Charlton Kings, Cheltenham, at the time a fairly new concept in horse training. The pool was hired out to trainers who would bring their horses over to use its facilities.

The previous year he made his first impression on the amateur jockeys' table, finishing the 1973/4 season in ninth place with twelve winners from 89 mounts.

Jim Wilson on the Michael Henriques-owned and trained Kelly's Hero at Cheltenham in the B.J. Angell Handicap Steeplechase for amateur riders, 24 October 1979. Jumping well at this point Wilson pulled the horse up before the sixteenth when it went lame, and T. Thomson Jones went on to win on Crofter. Also in this race were Miss D. Harris, pictured on the left on Rosevale Cottage and a very young Peter Scudamore (not pictured). (Courtesy of Bernard Parkin)

Never getting the backing of a big stable and always having to make his own way, the fact that Jim was ultimately so successful as an amateur must be put down to his own ability in the saddle.

In 1976 Wilson got his first ride in the Grand National on a horse called Thomond, a bay gelding that he had been riding all season without any success. In all their previous six races of the season which started at Cheltenham on 5 December 1975, they failed to better a finishing place of fifth. Unfortunately the Grand National was similarly uninspiring; at the first fence Wilson lost his irons and at the fourth they were brought down. Wilson would go on to feature in five Grand Nationals, the next one not until 1981 when Another Prospect fell at the eighth. In 1982 he partnered Rolls Rambler who got as far as the twenty-second but then refused and was seen to break a blood vessel. It wouldn't be until his partnership with Broomy Bank in 1984 that he would complete the course; of the 23 finishers and 40 runners he finished a very respectable eighth with the horse that had previously won him the Kim Muir at the Cheltenham Festival. His last Grand National would again be with Broomy Bank, and it would be the following year. Having failed to ride him all season Wilson got the ride for the great Aintree race but at the twenty-third of the thirty fences the two parted company and Jim Wilson's Grand National dream was over.

The first big win of his career came in the Cheltenham Festival of 1979, the season when he would go on to finish second in the amateurs' table with 20 winners. The third race of the first day of the Festival was the Coral Golden Handicap Hurdle Race Final and Jim was riding his mother-in-law's horse, Willie Wumpkins. In 1973 Willie Wumpkins won the Aldsworth Hurdle Race at the Cheltenham Festival, trained by Adrian Maxwell and ridden by P. Colville, then rather desperately lost his form. He went for a time to David Nicholson's yard, where at one time he became so ill that the trainer thought he would die. When the horse regained his health, Jane Pilkington herself took the responsibility of training him under permit, several vets having told her that he should be put down. She rode him every day, and once a week would take him to Jim's pool to swim, which became twice a week when races were impending.

Leading up to the Festival Jim Wilson had been given the ride on Willie Wumpkins in two of his three warm-up races. The first was on Boxing Day 1978 at Wolverhampton when they finished fourth in the Walsall Handicap Hurdle Race, then at the same track on 16 January they led briefly in the Chadsmoor Handicap Hurdle Race before fading and failed to finish in contention. Robin Dickin rode the horse in the Rendlesham Handicap Hurdle Race at Kempton Park on 24 February and came home fourth out of 24 runners – then it was time for Cheltenham.

Willie Wumpkins was aged eleven when Wilson was set to ride him in the 1979 Festival. The handicap weight was set at 10 stone 1 lb, but the jockey couldn't make it and so he put up 3 lb overweight. Clearly the public weren't impressed by

Jim Wilson at Cheltenham on the Jane Pilkington-owned and trained Willie Wumpkins, April 1980. In this race, the Early's of Witney George Duller Handicap Hurdle Race, they only managed to finish third, behind Patzrustler and Donnison. In the Festival of the previous month, however, they had won the Coral Golden Handicap Hurdle Final for the second successive year. (Courtesy of Bernard Parkin)

the horse's indifferent form and they started the race at odds of 25/1. Wilson always kept the horse in contention, never moving out of the first three, and then with three hurdles to jump he took him into the lead from where he determinedly carved out a winning margin of five lengths from second-placed Jonjo O'Neill – the reigning champion jockey who would win that season's Gold Cup on Alverton. The horse that O'Neill was riding was Little Owl, owned by Jim's aunt. Wilson retained the ride on Willie Wumpkins for the rest of the season but of the three races only impressed at Devon and Exeter, just over a week after Cheltenham, when they were beaten by three-quarters of a length in the Woodbury Handicap Hurdle Race.

The following season Jim Wilson was once again being asked to ride the ageing racehorse, starting with the Nicolet Instruments Handicap Hurdle Race at Cheltenham on 10 November. They failed to impress, finishing ninth. In fact in his next six races Willie Wumpkins' best result was a second at Chepstow in November in the Celtic Amateur Riders' Handicap Hurdle Race. Ironically it was one of the two occasions that Wilson wouldn't be riding the horse before the Festival; more ironically Wilson was on the winning horse that day when he brought the favourite Knockagin home twelve lengths clear for trainer Peter Cundell.

So when the Festival came round in 1980 Willie Wumpkins hadn't won a race since the previous March, but Jim Wilson had been showing consistency on other mounts and was once again on his way to finishing second in the amateur jockey ranks; his twenty-seven winners would be just two short of Oliver Sherwood's tally.

For the 1980 Festival a special trophy was inaugurated to be presented to the jockey who had the most winning rides during the three days. The Ritz Club Charity Trophy has in subsequent years been won by the best National Hunt jockeys riding: Peter Scudamore, John Francome, Jonjo O'Neill, Richard Dunwoody, Charlie Swan and Tony McCoy have all had their names engraved on it. The first to win the trophy with a tally of three winners, one on each day of the Festival, was A.J. Wilson.

The Kim Muir Memorial Challenge Cup for amateur riders on the Tuesday brought the first sweet smell of success when, partnered with Mrs J. Edwards' Good Prospect, Jim Wilson came home three lengths ahead of R. Treloggen on Midday Welcome, with N. Madden on Kilkilwell a further four lengths behind in third.

The following day he saddled Willie Wumpkins in the Coral Golden Handicap Hurdle Final. This time they were carrying an extra 6 lb in weight compared with the previous year, but started the race joint second favourites at odds of 10/1. Wilson brought the twelve-year-old home by a comfortable four lengths from King Neptune in second and Two Coppers in third. After a largely uneventful season for Willie Wumpkins he had yet again won the Coral Golden Handicap Hurdle Final, and in an impressive fashion. It was almost as if he had saved everything up for the big race and the big occasion.

The National Hunt Handicap Steeplechase on Thursday 13 March 1980 completed the trio of winners for Wilson. The Cheltenham-based amateur won the 3 mile, 1 furlong long race on Again The Same, a horse that he had ridden less than two weeks earlier to win the Cox Moore Handicap Steeplechase at Market Rasen. The winning margins at the Festival were six lengths to Current Gold in second and a further twenty lengths to third-placed Sweet September.

In four of the seven races that Willie Wumpkins featured in before the 1981 Festival he was partnered by Jim Wilson; in none of them did he threaten to turn any heads for his performance, and nor did he in the three races when Wilson wasn't on his back. But both jockey and horse were entered again for the Coral Golden Handicap Hurdle Final, and now at the grand old age of thirteen, Willie Wumpkins was attempting to make it three successive wins for horse, jockey and trainer. The 3/1 favourite for the race was Fauloon, but public confidence was such that even at thirteen and carrying a 10 stone 8 lb handicap Willie Wumpkins was installed as second favourite with odds of 13/2.

The race turned out to be a procession and the old horse stormed to the finish an incredible thirteen lengths clear of second-placed Wait And See. For an amateur jockey to win a Festival race once with a horse trained by a permit holder is a great accomplishment for all three parties; for it to be achieved three times in succession is and was a staggering result, especially when it must be considered that the resources available to normal trainers with horses in the race would greatly outweigh those that Jane Pilkington had at her disposal. Yet she brought on a horse in the autumn of its career to capture the races that really mattered. Willie Wumpkins was almost an enigma, saving his best efforts for the Cheltenham Festival three years running and yet showing nothing and achieving almost nothing in between. He certainly did not have the talent of other great hurdlers that have graced the turf at Cheltenham, but the way in which he was carefully trained and brought on by Jane Pilkington and then knowledgeably ridden by Jim Wilson earns him an enviable and deserved position in the annals of racing history.

At the beginning of the 1981 season Wilson and his brother Robin inherited the big, strong, six-year-old gelding Little Owl from their aunt, Bobbie Gundry, who had died just three days after the 1980 Cheltenham Festival. Peter Easterby had paid 2,300 guineas for the Irish-bred unbroken three-year-old Little Owl at the Doncaster Sales and then the horse proceeded, most often ridden by Jonjo O'Neill, to set National Hunt racing alight.

On 1 March 1978 Little Owl won the Harewood Novices' Division Two Hurdle Race at Wetherby by an impressive eight lengths and then went on to win his remaining two races of the season. The following season he won three of his seven races, the first being his first race of the season, the Coral Golden Handicap Hurdle Qualifier at Nottingham in December. The next four races he lost. For the first two he was partnered by Jonjo O'Neill, and Tim Easterby took over for the next two races without success. The barren spell ended when Jim Wilson took over the ride for his aunt, winning the last two races: at Market Rasen on 19 May 1979 in a three mile handicap hurdle race and then on 28 May the Headley Handicap Hurdle Race at Wetherby which they won by twenty lengths. For the 1979/80 season Jonjo O'Neill was back in the saddle for all four of the horse's races, of which they only lost the Sun Alliance Novices' Steeplechase at the Cheltenham Festival. So when the Wilson brothers inherited this fabulous horse he had won nine of his fourteen races in the previous three seasons, two of them with Jim himself in the saddle. Quite naturally they kept him in training with Peter Easterby, and even more naturally Jim Wilson took over on all the rides with his brother having the privilege of having his colours worn; red sleeves and green body with a white hoop round the

Jim Wilson on Little Owl on the way to winning the 1981 Cheltenham Gold Cup.
(Courtesy of Bernard Parkin)

Jim Wilson and Little Owl being led into the winner's enclosure, having just won the 1981 Gold Cup.
(Courtesy of Bernard Parkin)

midriff and red cap. During that first season of their co-ownership of Little Owl, the horse was unbeaten in all five of the races that he rode in, earning prize money of £77,348 – more than any other that season and putting R.J. Wilson as second only to Queen Elizabeth the Queen Mother in the winning owners' table; they also helped Peter Easterby clinch the trainers' championship for the third year running and aided Jim Wilson to accumulate a tally of 21 winners for the season.

The first victory for the Wilson brothers came at Doncaster on 20 December 1980 in the David M. Adams Developments Steeplechase over two miles and four furlongs; the race was never contested, with Little Owl winning by twenty lengths. Next came the Peter Marsh Handicap Steeplechase at Haydock on 24 January 1981. This time the distance was three miles, but again there was nothing to touch Little Owl and Wilson, who won by fifteen lengths. At Cheltenham on 31 January was the Tote Double Steeplechase which was a closer run race, but the horse still justified his odds of 8/11-on and won by six lengths. Victory number four was once again at Haydock, this time in the Timeform Steeplechase which with only four runners was never going to be anyone's but Little Owl's and Jim Wilson's; they won by twelve lengths and were perfectly poised for the final victory of the season that was by far the most important and would prove to be a hugely popular one in the Cheltenham area. It came on 19 March 1981, the day following Jim Wilson's amazing treble victory with Willie Wumpkins in the Coral Golden Handicap Hurdle Final, at Cheltenham in the Gold Cup.

A field of fifteen runners congregated at the starting post, among whom was the fabulous dual Champion Hurdle winner Night Nurse, the 1978 Gold Cup winner Midnight Court, Tied Cottage who had won the race the previous year only to have it taken away from him following a dope test, and Silver Buck who would actually win the race the following year: the latter was installed as favourite at 7/2, Night Nurse and Little Owl sharing second favourite at 6/1.

Tied Cottage set the initial pace until he fell at the sixth and Diamond Edge took over. Then from the tenth to the twentieth it was Night Nurse that was heading the field, but Jim Wilson was always in the following pack holding Little Owl up, riding a perfectly timed and ultimately excellently executed race. From two out he moved his steed into the lead, Silver Buck moving with him, then Silver Buck's stamina let him down and he slipped behind Night Nurse who began to rally. Running on well to the finishing line Little Owl took the race by one and a half lengths from Night Nurse. Silver Buck finished a tired ten lengths back in third. All of Cheltenham began to celebrate. Their local racing hero had won the race that hadn't been won by an amateur since 1947 when Richard Black won on Fortina, and only once before that, in 1927 when Lord Stalbridge's Thrown In won with the Hon. Hugh Grosvenor in the saddle. In victory Jim Wilson raised his whip to the heavens and thanked his departed aunt for leaving him and his brother such a marvellous horse.

The following season was a direct contrast for Little Owl, as he was afflicted by the virus and his racing suffered badly. Wilson still managed 21 winners which brought him to third in the amateur ranks, but Little Owl raced just four times and did nothing in any of them. His best finish was a fifth; in the others he fell, was pulled up and unseated his jockey.

Robin and Jim Wilson being presented with the Cheltenham Gold Cup by Lord and Lady Wyatt. (Courtesy of Bernard Parkin)

Then for the 1982/3 season Wilson and Little Owl were back to their winning ways. On 6 December at Nottingham they won the Last Chance Steeplechase, a race of only three runners which saw Peter Scudamore's mount Kalkashanndi trail in twelve lengths behind in second place. This was followed by a victory in the Tommy Whittle Steeplechase at Haydock on 15 December when they beat Bregawn (who would win the Gold Cup at the end of the season) by ten lengths in a two horse race. A distant fourth in the King George VI Chase won by John Francome on Wayward Lad, a fourth at Haydock and a third at Sandown were all that was left for the nine-year-old horse in that season and although he continued to race for another two seasons he never came close to achieving the wonderful form that he had shown in that first season in which the Wilson brothers took up ownership. He retired to Jim Wilson's stables in Charlton Kings, where he died and was buried in 1997.

Jim Wilson's last winner at the Cheltenham Festival was in 1984. It was his seventh as a jockey in the National Hunt's greatest stage. In the Kim Muir Memorial Challenge Cup for amateur riders, Jim Wilson was partnered with the 16/1 outsider Broomy Bank – the horse he would go on to ride in two Grand Nationals – owned by Captain J.M.G. Lumsden and trained by John Edwards at Ross-on-Wye. Just before the nineteenth and final fence in the three-mile chase, Wilson took his horse into the lead and once they had jumped successfully he drove the nine-year-old gelding to the finishing post, four lengths clear of Honourable Man, with Sicilian Answer a further one and a half lengths behind.

In 1985, having ridden as an amateur 205 winners, seven of them at the Cheltenham Festival including the Gold Cup, and appeared in five Grand

Jim Wilson's stables in Charlton Kings, Cheltenham.

Nationals, Jim Wilson retired from the saddle and took up a licence to train from his home at the base of Ham Hill in Charlton Kings, Cheltenham.

Within two years he was once again in the winners' enclosure at the Cheltenham Festival, this time in his capacity as a trainer, but the race that his horse had won was the very same one that Willie Wumpkins had had such control over, the Coral Golden Handicap Hurdle Final. Six-year-old Taberna Lord ridden by Luke Harvey was the winning horse, a horse that had come into the Wilson stables at the beginning of the 1986/7 season, having had some success with the trainer D.J. Moorhead the previous season under the ownership of Warwick Lodge Racing Limited. When Cheltenham owner Roger Jackson bought the horse it was Jim Wilson in whom he put his faith as a trainer.

The first race that Jim Wilson entered the horse in was the Newent Handicap Hurdle Race at Cheltenham on 6 December 1986. It was an inauspicious start – out of the thirteen runners he finished tenth with Bruce Dowling in the saddle. From then on Luke Harvey partnered the horse and by their third race together, following two fifth-placed finishes, they had proved victorious. That first victory was at Sandown in the Tote Jackpot Handicap Hurdle Race on 7 February 1987 and just over a month later on Wednesday 18 March it would be followed by a victory of far greater importance.

Claiming a valuable 4 lb allowance Luke Harvey took over the lead at the last fence from Peter Scudamore on the Martin Pipe-trained Sporting Mariner. He then rode the top-weighted 10/1 shot to the finishing line just one and a half lengths clear with Emo Forever a distant third, a further twelve lengths astray.

Seven years later Jim Wilson turned out the winner of another big race when Glenbrook D'Or won the 1994 Midlands National. Then, however, successes from his stables were few and far between with the yard particularly hit by the virus. After a barren period in which nothing seemed to go right for Jim Wilson, he turned out Wot No Gin for the Oak Conditional Jockeys' Handicap Steeplechase at Wincanton with Shane Kelly in the saddle. They took the race by half a length from Ekeus and the trainer had his first winner after 37 successive losers.

Maybe this is a sign that his small establishment of just fifteen horses is once more destined for success.

Further Reading

Collens, Rupert, *50 Cheltenham Gold Cups*, Sporting Garland Press, 1995
Fitzgeorge-Parker, Tim, *The Ditch on the Hill,* Simon & Schuster, 1991
Gill, Peter, *Cheltenham Races*, Sutton Publishing, 1997
Green, Reg, *National Heroes: the Aintree Legend*, Mainstream Publishing, 1997
Herbert, Ivor, *Winter's Tale*, Pelham Books, 1974
Holland, Anne, *Stride by Stride*, Macdonald, Queen Anne Press, 1989
Lee, Alan, *Cheltenham Racecourse*, Pelham Books, 1985
Lee, Brian, *Welsh Steeplechase Jockeys*, Cwmnedd Press, 1993
Munting, Roger, *Hedges and Hurdles*, J.A. Allen, 1987
Nicholson, David with Powell, Jonathan, *The Duke*, Hodder & Stoughton, 1995
Pitman, Richard, *Good Horses Make Good Jockeys,* Pelham Books, 1976
Tanner, Michael, *The Champion Hurdle*, Pelham Books, 1989
Welcome, John, *The Cheltenham Gold Cup*, Pelham Books, 1984
Welcome, John, *Fred Archer*, Lambourn, 1990

Index